The FORTUNE TELLERS

BLACK WATCH
New York

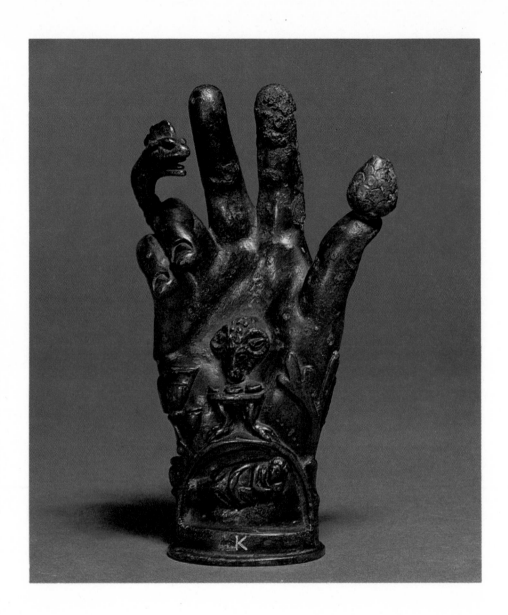

Published by Black Watch
Under arrangement with Ottenheimer Publishers Inc.
1632 Reistertown Road, Baltimore,
Maryland, 21208

Copyright © 1974 by Marshall Cavendish Publications Ltd.

Library of Congress Catalog Card Number 74 - 78296

ISBN 0 - 88486 - 004 - 3

Printed by Henri Proost, Turnhout, Belgium.

Introduction

Throughout time man has shown an insatiable curiosity about
himself and the universe in which he lives. Each age has made its own
advances in knowledge, achieved partial answers and insights. Today
we take great pride in scientific progress and technology, yet we still find
some of the most profound questions left unanswered.
Perhaps we sense that no system provides a complete and satisfying
explanation of life; besides, modern technology has often had the
effect of alienating human beings from their world.
Fortune tellers have survived throughout the history of the human race.
They are people who possess special ways of investigating the
world, whose tools have been as familiar as tea-leaves and strange as
rune sticks. These gifts have been handed down across the centuries,
living side by side with all the developments in other fields of
knowledge. Nowadays, more and more people are becoming
interested in the old lore, and the people who practise the art of
divination are once more coming into their own.
In *The Fortune Tellers* we not only see these people at work, but also
the various methods which they employ. Everyone has questions to
ask, and we show you how these gifted individuals set about answering
them. How do numbers affect our lives for instance, and are there
really such things as magic mirrors? What insights are revealed by
reading the Tarot, and can the I Ching system reveal the future?
This beautifully illustrated book is packed with fascinating information
about the art of divination, an art which is still vital and relevant to
the modern age.

Editor: Yvonne Deutch
Compiler: Francoise Strachan
Design: Jill Moore/Frank Landamore
Cover: Peter Rauter
Picture Research: Caroline Lucas

Contents

Preparation for Divination. 6-14
Francoise Strachan

Numerology. 15-29
Richard Deutch

I Ching. 30-44
Ashton Brown

How to Read Hands. 45-59
Jo Sheridan

The Runes. 60-74
Athene Williams

The Crystal. 75-89
Athene Williams

The Tarot for Life. 90-104
Richard Gardner

Tasseography. 105-119
Katherine Gray

Radiesthesia and Dowsing. 120-128
Katherine Gray

PREPARATION ❖FOR❖ DIVINATION

It must be remembered that divination is a great and powerful art, and there are numerous ways of recognising signs of divinity radiating through nature. Some techniques of divination are highly sophisticated and almost scientific, and others are so amazingly simple that even an intuitive child could understand. Before embarking on any divinatory techniques it is absolutely essential to ground one's whole being in the knowledge of truth, and to seek protection and guidance from the angelic beings and spirits that are constantly with us. Because of our

highly powered rate of living we take in all sorts of vibrations that affect our physical as well as our psychic bodies. Our bodies are miniature universes, and everything about us is a living symbol of ourselves. Once we are in harmony and in direct contact with the inner God-Power, then it is quite natural to be able to read the

Below: *Because the body and the mind are bombarded by all kinds of external influences, it is necessary for the practising diviner to cleanse himself of all impurities before practising his art.*

Above left: *Nearly everything in nature, even leaves, can tell the diviner something.* **Above right:** *A Buddhist meditation garden, which is ideal for achieving inner peace.*

living symbols in nature. Divination is a very ancient and sacred science, and should at all times be treated as such. If you want to read cards at a party just for fun or to gain popularity, or to learn the *I Ching* because you think that it is a fashionable thing to do, then by all means do it. But if you find something out that you did not really want to know about in the first place, or if you happen to tell someone something that upsets them so much that they want to commit suicide — then naturally be prepared to accept the consequences. On the other hand if you want to become a serious diviner treat it with reverence, then you will get all the help from the spirits and angels you need.

Total Cleansing

As our physical and psychic bodies are constantly bombarded with external vibrations, before embarking on any form of divination it is vital to cleanse oneself properly from all impure influences. If you are divining outside, and it is a lovely sunny day allow the sun to shine on your upturned face for about fifteen minutes and imagine all the impurities in your psyche going into the ground. Or if it is windy, imagine all the impurities blowing away in the wind. Creative imagination and the divine will, working together, always get excellent results, for one always complements the other. If you are divining indoors then use a purificatory incense to cleanse the room and also yourself. Frankincense and Assafoetida burnt together on a piece of charcoal, make very potent purifiers. Use proportionately more Frankincense on the charcoal, and just a little piece of Assafoetida.

Ideally it is best to take one's clothes off and put a small bowl of burning incense on the ground, and then make contact with the divine powers of your choice. The Father-Mother God to cleanse your physical body, and also all the psychic bodies so that you may be worthy of divining accurately. Then walk around the burning incense in a circle seven times for each of the bodies. As you do this mention the name of the body that is being purified: the physical, etheric, vital, the astral (or emotional) body, the mental, the causal (or spiritual body).

Check with the Pendulum

When you have done this then step over the burning incense three times and back again, so that the fumes will permeate every part of your body. When this is done you could put on a clean robe before embarking on the next step. It is advisable to learn to use the pendulum because this can be exceedingly useful. You can ask whether all impure influences have been removed. If the answer is positive then proceed with the divining, but if it is negative then ask the pendulum if the remaining influences can be burnt out. If the answer is yes, then get a piece of wire, and a tiny piece of tissue paper and place it on the top of the wire. Then concentrate hard, and imagine all the remaining negative influences collecting on the tissue paper; then burn it completely. When you have done this, then check with the pendulum again and find out if there are still any remaining dregs. If so, then continue to burn little bits of tissue paper until all harmful negativity has been removed.

All this is necessary, because if there are any impurities in the psyche, the divining could naturally be adversely influenced. So it is really important to get all negativities removed first, especially if one is trying to help another person. This paper burning technique should be effective to remove any psychic alien influences. But when they are removed, remember not to leave them lingering in the room to re-attach themselves. Ask the angelic beings to take away these influences, before doing anything else. Or imagine a blue sphere and visualise all these black specks being absorbed into it. This usually takes a few minutes but you will feel really cleansed and bright afterwards. If you are divining for a friend, it would be advisable for them to also go through the same purificatory ritual if they are with you, otherwise you could easily pick up their psychic debris. With divining one obviously picks up the good together with the bad but there is little point in taking on an unnecessary psychic load.

When you have finished divining, it is advisable to burn some more incense and purify the room with consecrated water, because when people are discussing their problems it is only too easy for them to leave negative or disturbed thought forms about. If you happen to sleep in the same room that you are divining in, you could experience a very restless night. All these precautions should be seriously considered and should if possible be carried out. It is advisable not to eat a large meal before divining, as this is inclined to desensitize one. This is, of course, if you want to achieve really excellent results.

To become a really good diviner one should daily contact one's inner God-Power by doing a short meditation of about fifteen to twenty minutes. This will help to clear some of the 'clattering thoughts', and gradually bring about a direct contact with the Centre of Power. By being in constant contact with this terrific force, and by quietly listening for guidance instead of thinking that one knows it all, then one could, with a little patience and humility, become an excellent diviner. Gradually a strong relationship builds up with the inner powers, if one constantly keeps connected, and eventually it becomes a total rapport. If one really lets the divine motivate one's being then the language of divination becomes the norm, and 'supernatural' things become amazingly natural. They were only thought of as super-natural in the first place, because people were never connected in to the inner power house of the universe, viewing the world superficially.

The Spirits of Objects

With divination literally anything you care to think about can tell you something. A bunch of sticks, stars, a flight of birds, the direction of the winds, a few pebbles, a handful of earth, itching on the body, movements of animals, physical organs, orange peel, candles, even the appear-

Right: *Patterns and shapes throughout nature give the diviner hints at inner reality. Here a beautifully marked and coiled snake reveals its own set of hidden messages.*

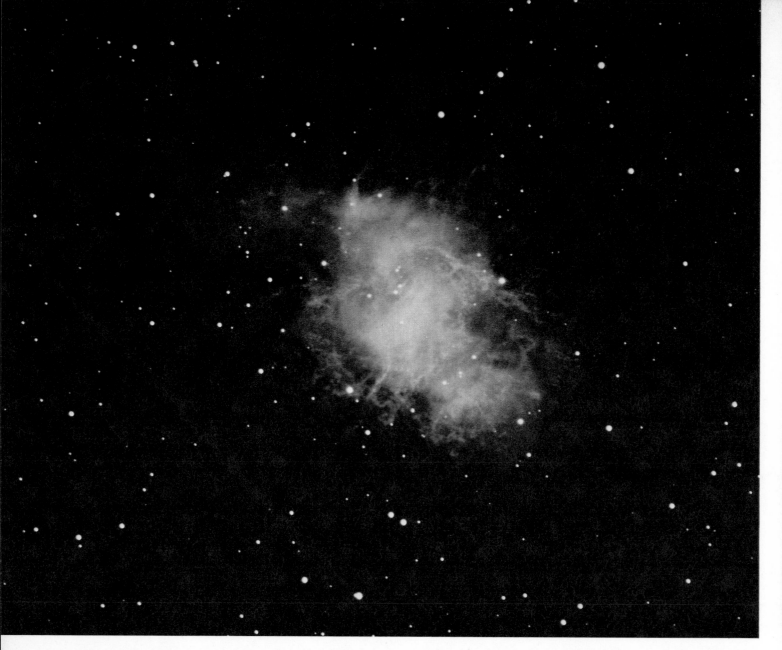

ances of snakes at certain places, deformities, symptoms in diseases, shadows, and even the peculiarities of new born children and animals, to name but a few. When the inner power house is really operating then you will naturally be in tune with everything else in nature. Every object will speak to you in its own special language. If your personal power is motivated by real loving-ness then everything in the outer universe will feel this love and naturally respond to it, and will spontaneously yield its secret. If you would first prefer to work with one specific object then you must contact its guardian spirit and seek its aid. If you decide to use sticks, for example, then con-tact the spirits of the trees in your meditations and ask for the right set of sticks to come along to help you. If you don't like meditating then go out and contact the trees yourself, and if you are sincere then the right sticks will come to you.

Above: *The sky at night has always attracted the interest and wonder of man. The diviner seeks to be in touch with the stars and the majestic power of the universe.*

They will be worth waiting for.

When they come bless them, and talk to them regularly. Build up a harmonious relationship with them, so that they positively vibrate with energy and power. All the atoms and molecules are moving about in sticks as they are in anything else, and their potency will increase if they are treated lovingly and with respect. When you come to use them for divining they will be positively alive and will be able to speak to you, and when you and the sticks have become one, when you divine they will simply be an extension of yourself and they will be used to re-affirm your own inner knowledge.

Above left: *Formations in clouds and*
Above: *the sudden appearance of a flock of birds in the sky can have magical significance.*

Divining with Animal Livers

One of the most incredible forms of divination was practised by the Babylonians in the fifth century, B.C., and this was the art of divining by using the liver of animals. The Babylonians firmly believed that the liver was a sacred organ, and that it was in fact the seat of the soul, incorporating the emotional, mental, and spiritual aspects of man. The idea was quite unusual because other cultures believed that the heart

Left: *The Babylonians regarded the liver rather than the heart as the centre of life. Here is a liver divided into special sections for divination purposes.*

was the sacred centre. Each section of the liver corresponded to a different aspect of man. The diviners were specially trained in the temples. The teachers used models of liver made out of clay, and sometimes even used real liver. The symbolical structure of the liver was a highly complex science. The liver is divided into four lobes, and no doubt these represented the four elements, and the fourfold nature of man, among numerous other things. The surface was then divided into fifty squares, and there were also additional complex sections. Even the layers within the liver held a special esoteric significance. The diviners were able to tell much by the actual condition of each separate section. To the expert eye the sacred symbol of the liver became a living replica which opened the doors of the past, present and future. But the Babylonian priests considered this a very specialised and sacred form of divination which had been invented by the Gods and not by mere mortals.

Divining with a Candle

But for practical purposes it is easier to use simpler methods — like candles, for instance, a lighted candle being a dynamic symbol of life. Candles can be used for numerous purposes, but they are ideal if you want to know how long someone is going to live; and you must of course want to know the correct answer for a *very* good reason. The motive behind the action is all important; and if the motive is really extraordinary, then of course the answer will also be extraordinary. So be prepared. Buy a large candle, and rub consecrated oil on it thinking of the person. Then ritually bless it with salt and water, and quietly entreat the angelic forces to put the candle out at the correct year. Put markings all down one side of the candle to indicate the number of years. When it is dry, place it somewhere that is completely free of draughts. Say out loud very positively that you wish to know how long the person is going to live and state the reason why you want to know. If you have difficulty in lighting the candle, then think carefully about your motives again and make quite sure that they are quite genuine. If the candle blows out immediately, then death is imminent (or less tragic, you have a faulty wick)! But do not forget to make a note of how many marks you have made on the candle otherwise when you come to count the remaining

notches when the candle has gone out you could make a very nasty mistake.

Skulls, Leaves and Sticks

There are of course many other quite fascinating forms of divination, and so really one has an endless choice. Botanomancy: sounds quite impressive doesn't it? But this simply means burning branches and leaves to get the required answers. If you prefer skulls why not practice Cephalomancy? This would entail finding the skull of a donkey or a goat, and could be rather difficult to obtain. But if you are lucky enough to find one and talk to it nicely, it will then disclose all the things you wish to know. You would probably find it much easier practising Dendromancy, and this would be ideal during the Christmas holidays because all you need is oak and mistletoe to get your answers. Divination from leaves is quite fun: Sycomancy. You have to write your personal request on them, and the slower that they dry up the more positive your answer will be; provided of course that you do not practise in a hot room! Xylomancy is finding pieces of wood at random and interpreting them according to their shape. Or you could place pieces of wood on the fire, and draw your own conclusions from which piece happens to burn first. However I think that one of the most enjoyable forms of divination is watching clouds racing across the sky. If you sincerely ask questions of the clouds you will find an answer forming itself into a picture in intricate detail. Sometimes one is specially privileged and sees the Gods on their day off enjoying the daylight, or talking to one another in slow motion and when they have finished their conversation they collapse into one another in laughter.

Divining with Water

Water divining is still greatly used and is much cheaper and just as effective as a crystal ball. The ancients used this simple method to see into the future, because special powers have always been attributed to water and it has always been acknowledged as the sacred source of life. The early diviners used a specially chosen vessel made either in gold or refined copper, and some of these can be seen in museums today. But any container can be used, but should be specially consecrated and kept for this purpose and wrapped in silk when not in use to seal off any adverse influences. Consecrate some cold clear water then pour it into your vessel. The enquirer should then ask his special question directly to the Spirit of the Water. At the same time the diviner has inwardly contacted the water powers and spirits, and can do this by spontaneously reciting prayers and invocations quite softly but with direct resolution, vibrating power behind the words spoken. In your own words ask the powers to reveal themselves to the the enquirer in the water, then gradually pictures will build up and the future will be revealed. Sometimes black water or even ink has been used, as some people claim that this gives a much clearer picture. When the divining has been completed the Spirit of the Water should be graciously thanked, and all the protecting spirits. For they really like to be thanked, and if one ignores this fact they may not do the job quite so effectively the next time.

The Orris Root
The Orris Root is also excellent for divining if made into a pendulum. This special root is sacred to Aphrodite and also, interestingly enough, to Lucifer. It should be suspended by a long thread, approximately 12in.—14in. One uses this in the same way as one would use a pendulum made out of any other material. But the root is alive and holds such potent properties that it may well be preferred to using a wooden,

Below: *Divination involving the examination of skulls is known as Cephalomancy. The hoard of skulls shown here is from the Citadel of skulls, where hundreds of monks' bones are buried.*

ivory, or silver pendulum. This root also symbolises love and wisdom, so automatically responds readily to a sympathetic and powerful diviner. Geomancy is a well known form of divining and is still used widely today. It is easy to obtain handfuls of sand or earth, and then to throw it on to the ground, and read the symbols. It is certainly a more spacious way of divining than tea-leaf reading, and equally effective. But it does depend very much on where you happen to be at the time. The earth or sand falls into all sorts of unusual shapes, and once the Spirit of the Earth or Sand has been contacted the communication will be simple yet dynamic. The pat-

Above: *The lighted candle is frequently regarded as a dynamic symbol of life. It is possible to use a specially marked and consecrated candle to find out how long someone will live.*

terns may reveal themselves in zodiacal symbols, numbers, shapes, stars, or animals. The possibilities are simply limitless. Making dots at random in slightly wet sand is equally effective, also dots with a pen on paper. When creative visualization is at work coupled with true magical power, then direct contact is made with all the force in nature, and one is well on the way to becoming an excellent diviner.

NUMEROLOGY

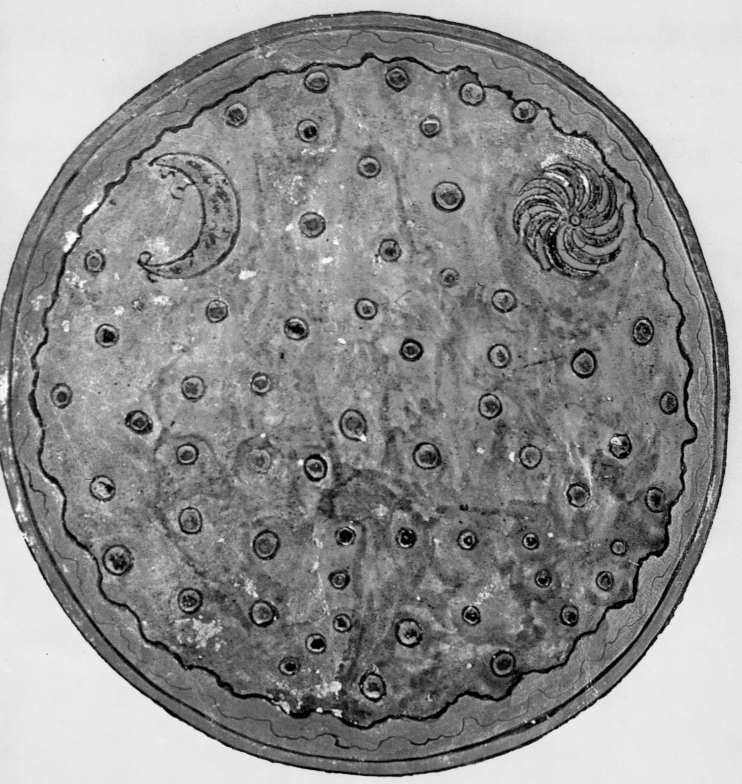

Numbers govern all things in the universe from the greatest to the smallest.

'We know infinitesimally little of the material universe. Our detailed knowledge is so contemptibly minute, that it is hardly worth reference, save that our shame may spur us to increased endeavour. Such knowledge as we have got is of a very general and abstruse, of a philosophical and almost magical character. This consists principally of the conceptions of pure mathematics. It is, therefore, almost legitimate to say that pure mathematics is our link with the rest of the universe and with 'God'.'

Aleister Crowley,
Magick in Theory and Practice

Above: *Many other methods of fortune telling, like this 18th century woman using cards, are also effective, although they are far less rich in imagery and symbolism than numerology.*

In an essay of this length I don't intend to delve more than superficially into the history of numerology, nor to speculate as to why it does in fact work. Suffice it to say that the principle behind numerology is this: we find numbers, measure, governing all things in the universe; were this not the case, the vast multiplicity of heavenly bodies we observe in the sky would have collided into a fiery mass billions of years ago; and it seems reasonable to assume that numbers should have their influence on terrestial matters as well. When, on trying out this theory, we come up with startlingly consistent results, we must conform to the rule of science which states that the simplest and most comprehensive explanation for a phenomenon is the correct one.

The Systems

There are various systems of number and letter equivalents, and you should try them all on the names of a few persons you know well in order to decide which system makes most sense to you. As with any means of divination — tarot, pendula, runes, the crystal ball — numerology is most useful as a key to your own Greater Consciousness, a very small fraction of which is ever used by the average human being. One extremely competent clairvoyant I know used to make amazing forecasts for strangers by reading tea leaves at the bottom of a cup they had drunk; now that fewer people drink tea, she uses instant coffee instead. By the same token, any system of numerology, ancient or modern, is right if it is right for *you*. The tarot is a very ancient and sacred code, a symbolical language unto itself, but many people tell fortunes and even cast spells using ordinary playing cards. (On the other hand, they're denying themselves a rich source of imagery and symbolism, both excellent aids to divination, and a magical treasure hoard of correspondences, but if they get the results they are after then method is relatively unimportant.) So it's best to experiment a little before settling down to one system or the other; although I feel dutybound to point out what I believe to be essential advantages in using the Hebrew system, don't let me raise any self-doubts in the reader if he finds he gets better results with something a little more up to date.

The modern system, sometimes, for some

reason, called Pythagorean, is this:

1	2	3	4	5	6	7	8	9
A	B	C	D	E	F	G	H	I
J	K	L	M	N	O	P	Q	R
S	T	U	V	W	X	Y	Z	

It contains, as the Hebrew system does not, the number 9, and is, as you can see, simplicity itself. A very effective version of the Hebrew system is put forth by Richard Cavendish:

1	2	3	4	5	6	7	8
A	B	C	D	E	U	O	F
I	K	G	M	H	V	Z	P
Q	R	L	T	N	W		
J		S		X			
Y							

In this system, Hebrew equivalents of English letters are used throughout, except in cases where the English has no exact parallel in Hebrew. The system does not contain the number 9, for reasons which needn't concern us here (nobody's quite sure what they are, anyway). Cavendish points out that there is no alphabetical equivalent for the Hebrew 9 in English; others more mystically inclined have submitted that the ancient Hebrews recognized 9 as a particularly sacred and powerful number and hence decided to leave it out — certainly they're right on the first point. Another excellent system is the one which Isidore Kozminsky gives as a simplification of that propounded by S. L. 'MacGregor' Mathers, the master magician.

1	2	3	4	5	6	7	8
A	B	G	D	E	U	O	F
I	C	L	M	H	V	Z	P
J	K	S	T	N	W		
Q	R		X				
Y							

This system, also Hebraic, differs from that of Cavendish with regard to C and X. Cavendish, quite naturally and sensibly in my opinion, regards C as roughly equivalent in vibration with G; Kozminsky reckons C as 2, no doubt identifying it with the Hebrew *caph*, 11, which adds to 2. Something in my nature will not allow me to equate Hebrew *beth* with *gimel* (B with G), so I personally opt for Cavendish on this

question. X, however, is more open to debate. Cavendish equates it with Greek *xi*, 60, admitting that 'some numerologists count X as 5, presumably because it resembles the dot-symbol for 5, . . ! In fact, X is more traditionally

. .

counted as 5 and, to me at least, this makes more sense in practice. If we analyze the name Alexander, for example, according to both systems, we find the following:

A	L	E	X	A	N	D	E	R
1	3	5	6	1	5	4	5	2

32

5

DIGITAL NO.	5
HEART NO.	3
PERSONALITY NO.	2

(Cavendish)

A	L	E	X	A	N	D	E	R
1	3	5	5	1	5	4	5	2

31

4

DIGITAL NO.	4
HEART NO.	3
PERSONALITY NO.	1

(Mathers/Kozminsky)

As you'll soon be able to work out for yourself, counting X as 6 we come up with an Alexander who is brilliant, restless, impetuous, fond of betting and fond of a drink, sexually polymorphous if not perverse. His heart number indicates he is attractive and has natural good luck; he may be a bit flighty, however, and over anxious as to what others think of him. The number 2 indicates a certain femininity in his public image; he is careful, politic, a bit bitchy, sometimes wishy-washy in the tradition of Charlie Brown. A pleasant enough fellow, if you stay on the right side of him and he stays on the right side of himself. Counting X as 5, we get a very different Alexander. He is essentially a builder, a layer of foundations; creative, but not on paper or canvas — in *fact*. This is his life's pattern, his destiny. Under the surface, however, he combines some of the character of the previous Alexander: magnetic, favoured of the gods, utterly spontaneous in his actions, he sees himself as easily succeeding where lesser men would fail. This attitude carries over into his personality number, 1, which is the face he presents to the world. 1 is the number of the god figure, uncompromisingly the leader, haughty, not always in control of his own massive ego, this Alexander is a single-tracked adventurer into the Unknown. He does not take criticism gracefully — in fact, he's unlikely to take it at all — and once he's made up his mind there's no changing it. Not nearly so happy or pleasant-natured as the other Alexander, he is often lonely. The god man.

If we apply these very different analyses to history's most famous Alexander, the man who spread and established Hellenic culture throughout the known world (thus giving us much of the basis of our own culture), an outstanding general and excellent administrator and yet inwardly a most erratic, unhappy and sexually confused individual — a man who did in fact declare himself a god — we find that the second analysis, in which X is counted as 5, makes a good deal more sense in this one instance. But you will be able to decide for yourself, after very little practice, which system of numerology works best for you. As a beginner you are, however, most strongly cautioned to *stick to the system you choose*. Later on, as your intuitions are sharpened, you will be able to combine them; but for the moment any shilly-shallying between systems will only produce rationalised half-truths, self-deception and incongruous, or even dangerous, mistakes. Any given system can work for any person, but it is absolutely essential to be consistent at first.

My own choice of systems is the one which Cavendish gives, with X counting as 5. My preference for the Hebrew is based, theoretically, on the fact that so much of our knowledge of numerology comes from the Kabala, the ancient Hebrew encyclopedia of mysticism, and so many useful analogies appear between numerology and the tarot, which some say is an anagram for Torah, that to use any system not based on Hebrew seems deliberately self-limiting. In practice, I prefer the Hebrew system because it is the only one which yields results that are useful to me. The student will find he can have lots of fun

Below: *Alexander the Great was creative and a builder according to one number system.*
Right: *One system sees Jesus Christ as attractive, another as intolerably ambitious.*

trying out the various systems on people he knows, or famous names; Jesus Christ, for example, is either an amazingly attractive and vibrant religious enthusiast with an essentially migratory nature (Hebrew system) or an intolerably ambitious man with more of a tinge of religious mania (modern) — a Superstar, indeed. Soon the student will find the system he feels most at home with, and for the moment at least, let him stick with it till he finds something that works better.

The Meanings Of The Numbers

If the systems of number-and-letter equivalents vary — there are in fact many more, and some a good deal more complicated, than the ones I've given here — the actual meanings of the numbers, drawn largely from the Kabala and astrology, are more generally agreed upon. However, yet another word of caution: the *interpretations* of these meanings can differ from numerologist to numerologist. If your digital number is 4, for example, you may consider that you are literally and figuratively a 'square'. You may also, as your friends will be grateful to find out when they're in a tight spot, be a 'brick'; and before you consider committing suicide over your digital number it might be well to reflect that you share yours with Alexander the Great. Some numbers are considered favourable, some are not; but it is well to remember that everything in existence has its positive and negative aspects. I tend to agree with Louise Huebner, 'Official Witch of Los Angeles' (witch or no witch, she's a whizz at numerology), when she says that any number is your 'lucky' number if you understand and use it rightly.

The Number One

1, as we have seen, is the number of the god figure. The number of the Creator, the primal generator of all things, it is very powerful indeed, and its sign is the sun. If your digital number is 1 you are at best an enormously forceful and at worst an annoyingly obstinate individual; but one thing's certain, you are an individual. 1's want to rise to the top and stay there. They will brook no opposition, and their word is law. They are willing to try new ideas, pursue untrodden paths, and let nothing stand in their way. 1's have the archetypal One-Track Mind; and unless their feelings of superiority are balanced by a sense of humour — which it is difficult for them to extend to themselves — and sufficient intelligence, humanity and talent to justify their massive egos, they can be totally incorrigible, like senile army commanders. They are either remarkable persons or crashing bores.

The Number Two

2 has been much maligned as the number of division (the Pythagoreans are said to have regarded 2 as no number at all, merely a confused unity) and hence duality, the separation of man from God. Thus the legend that Eve, second wife of Adam and the second human being, tempted her husband and caused humanity to be deprived of its heritage in the Garden of Eden. Those whose digital number is 2 do in fact tend to exhibit certain feminine characteristics; in contrast to our leonine 1's they are naturally reticent and more willing to compromise in order to keep the peace. By nature they may seem placid, ingratiating; but don't let them fool you — like a slumbering cat, they're plotting all the time. They prefer to achieve their ends by stratagem rather than frontal assault — hence that deceptive self-effacing quality. Marilyn Monroe, as Cavendish points out, was a 2.

On the positive side, 2's can be genuinely sweet persons, male and female. They have a quiet side to their natures which is most appealing. 2 is the number of polarity, of opposites: there is no male without female, no positive without negative, no birth or fruition without some form of separation followed by union. I think it's true that the 2-nature becomes good or evil *in combination* with other factors, both in the total personality of the person himself and in his relationship with the outer world. 2 is ruled, of course, by the ever-feminine moon.

The Number Three

3s are sparkling characters. Attractive, full of life, jacks of all trades but unlikely to bother mastering one unless it comes to them quite naturally — as it may well do — they seem to draw good fortune to them whatever they attempt. The 3's intellect and wit are unusually acute; he is conversant on a multitude of subjects, and speaks with charm and grace. People tend naturally to follow him, but he prefers to remain unattached. A natural winner, flighty as a sparrow. Jesus Christ, according to the Hebrew system, is a 3.

The darker side of the 3's nature stems from his independence: he is inordinately proud, and detests obligations of any kind. Relying as he does on the admiration of others, he is at once too independent and not self-reliant enough.

The Number Four

4, like 2, is a number which most numerologists find inauspicious, regarding the 4-nature as dull, plodding, lacking in imagination, self-righteous and respectable to a fault: the typical 'square' father of the heroine in a 'generation gap' musical. 4's in general are unlikely to come up with any great ideas of Western man; they are not terribly creative, and resent and distrust those who are.

At its highest level, 4 is the number of foundation, an essential number for the Kabalist as it represents the 4-lettered name of God. It represents not only the Tetragrammaton but the four elements, the four seasons, the four winds, the four angels Michael, Gabriel, Raphael and Uriel, and incidentally, the four cardinal points of the magic circle. All creation manifests itself through the number 4. The 4-nature at best is a 'pillar of society' and capable of making a positive contribution.

The Number Five

5's make excellent, if not overly faithful, bedmates. They are extremely attractive, energetic persons, and often their energy is sexual. Like 3's, they are clever and charming; they dislike staying in one spot too long, and are apt to be done with you before you've even started with them. Whatever their profession in life, their interests and talents are multiple, and they skip from one subject to the next like a stone across water. However, beware: like their cousins the 3's they are independent, resent restrictions or responsibilities of any kind, and share the tendency of 1's to satisfy their own cravings, even at the expense of others. Quick as foxes, 5's may be dangerous to know but great fun to watch.

The Number Six

6 is the number of domesticity, harmony, and even temper. Fair-minded and slow to anger, much in contrast with the 5-nature, by the way, 6's make excellent wives and husbands, just,

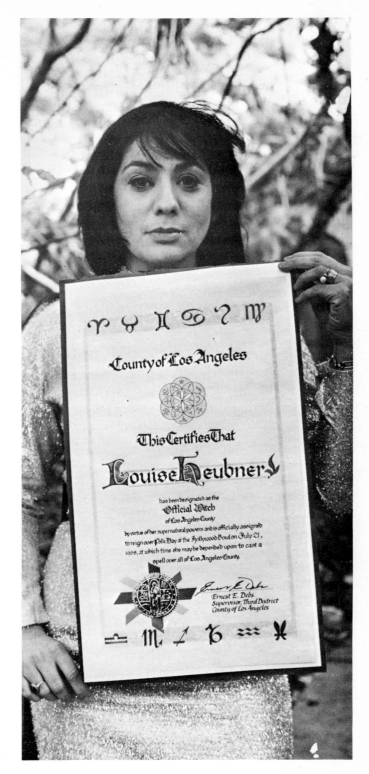

Above: *Louise Huebner proudly displays the certificate appointing her official witch of Los Angeles county, awarded the day she cast a spell to increase sexual vitality in the county.*
Overleaf left: *The Evangelists, pictured in wheels bearing the forms of a man, lion, bull and eagle, are governed by the number 4.*
Overleaf right: *The moon, related to number 2.*

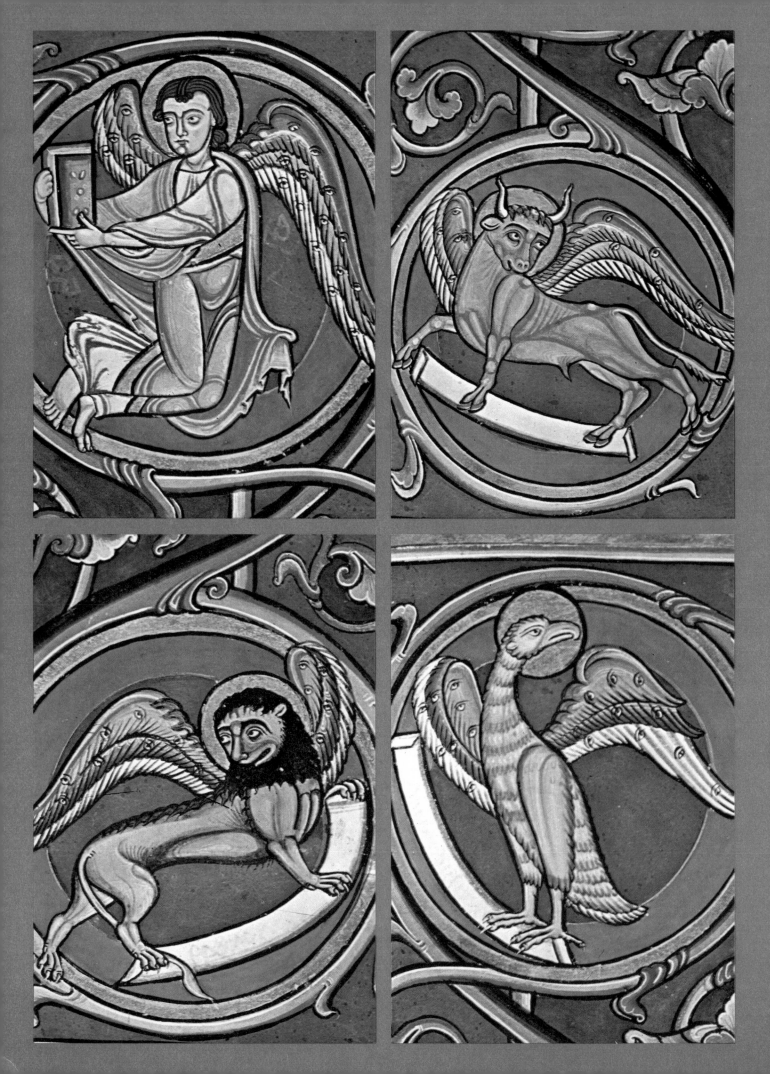

conscientious parents and good loyal friends. In a pinch, you can trust the 6 to stand by his principles (or by you while you stand up for yours). Clean-living, often fun to be with, 6's make excellent mates if you can put up with their sometimes 4-like squareness, their tendency to gossip and occasionally appalling smugness. At best they're like a sunny day, and indeed, 6 is a number of the sun.

The Number Seven

7 is traditionally a number of mystery, and popular numerologists invariably hint that it is the number of occultists. In fact, I know of only two occultists whose digital number is 7: my own teacher, and Jo Sheridan, who is writing the section on palmistry for this book. 7's are indeed secretive creatures, stand-offish, disciplined, haughty, mysterious. The 7 is often hiding something, an uncommon number of actors' names add to 7, such as Marlon Brando — and often as not that something is unhappiness, world-weariness and disillusionment; hence the *noli me tangere* attitude. Howard Hughes, whose dislike of publicity has made him world-famous, is a 7. 7's are often bitter people, disdainful and sarcastic as well.

The Number Eight

8's share with 1's the absolute determination to succeed in life; they are tough, single-minded in purpose, and often a bit dogmatic regarding their methods: the word *commander* adds to 8. Hard-minded individuals, they are rarely inspired like 3's, 6's or 9's, and success does not come easily to them, nor indeed need it come at all. But win or lose, they do it big. The 8 works tenaciously for his position, and once he's attained it he's not going to let it go; 8's are often miserly — the classic example in literature is Ebeneezer Scrooge — and like 7's, they hold no corner on the world's quota of happiness. The 8-nature is basically materialistic.

The Number Nine

9's couldn't be more different. 9 in the tarot is the number of the Hermit: wise counsellor, spiritual leader, seeker after and teacher of truth. 9s are idealists in the highest sense of the word, and are often fully capable of realizing those ideals in action. They are strongly passionate individuals, possessed of durable wills and highly charged emotions. Impulsive in the extreme, they are natural romantics and occasionally tend to lose sight of the particular while focusing on the ideal: hence they can give offence without even noticing, and be almost 1-like when you criticize or disagree with them. It's not easy to keep up with a 9, or to match his love if he loves you. Remarkable people, though.

Only two more numbers will suffice the beginner, and rarely does the experienced numerologist encounter them. 11's and 22's are truly *exceptional* persons, genuine masters, near-geniuses. I have met only one 11 in my life, and his mind races so swiftly from one abstract concept to the next that it's difficult for him to conduct an ordinary conversation. I have never met a 22. In most instances, as we shall see in a minute, 11 and 22 reduce to mundane 2 and 4, respectively.

Using The Numbers

Take a clean sheet of paper, and on it write the name of a person whom you wish to 'read'. Under the letters of the name write the corresponding numbers for each letter, according to whatever system you are using. For example, let us analyze the name Richard Jenkins using the Hebrew system.

R	I	C	H	A	R	D		J	E	N	K	I	N	S
2	1	3	5	1	2	4		1	5	5	2	1		5	3

Now add the numbers together in the first and second names. Richard adds to 18, Jenkins to 22. (It is traditional to add only from left to right, but if your addition is weak, it's well to double check by adding backwards; a mistake in addition is the one thing to avoid at all costs.) Rather than undertake at once the formidable task of dealing in numbers above 9, we shall reduce each number until we have a single digit, by combining the digits of every number: thus 18 (1+8) becomes 9, and 22 (2+2), except in unusual cases, becomes 4. With the information we now have we can determine the following about Richard Jenkins:

DIGITAL NUMBER. This is the 'essential' number, the sum total of the man himself and what his life will be like. It is only completely accurate when considered in the light of the personality and heart numbers, but it's not uncommon to hear persons remark, 'Oh, he's a 4'. just as they might say, 'She's a Virgo'. To obtain a complete picture of the person a good deal more astrological information is required than just the sun sign, though the sun sign is most important. Similarly, if we could obtain only one key number in assessing character it would have to be the digital number.

HEART NUMBER. This is the indicator of the inner man, the person as he sees or would like to see himself, what newspaper columnists would describe — somewhat inaccurately — as the 'real' man. It indicates secret aspirations too.

PERSONALITY NUMBER. This number indicates the outer man.

TO OBTAIN THE DIGITAL NUMBER, combine the sums of all names which the person uses and reduce to a single digit.

TO OBTAIN THE HEART NUMBER, combine the sums of all the vowels in the name. 'Y' follows the rule of English grammar which states that it is only counted as a vowel if there are no other vowels in the word; thus y is a vowel in Lynn, but a consonant in Lynne.

TO OBTAIN THE PERSONALITY NUMBER combine the sums of all consonants in the name.

It is important to use the person's essential name: i.e., the one with which he most identifies; otherwise the result will be a distortion of character. The reader need only try this with a few persons he knows well to see the point: if you have known a Tony intimately for some years and never heard him call himself anything else, it is folly to analyze him as Anthony. On the other hand, nicknames are not allowed. Rule-of-thumb is the only one we can apply here. Married women will have a fascinating time analyzing their maiden as opposed to married names: the difference will indicate how their marital relationship has changed them. A combination of both names, such as Mary Evans Jones, will be enlightening as well if it is ever used. Middle names should only be included for the same reason.

Kabalists up to the present time believe that changing a person's name will change his character, and, since character is fate, his destiny as well: it is common practice to change the name of a sick man as an aid to his recovery. (This sheds some light on the biblical incident in which Yahweh informs Abram that 'henceforth he shall be called Abraham'.) In a minute we shall see what happened to Richard Jenkins when he changed his surname to Burton. But for the moment, let's have a look at Richard Jenkins.

Richard Jenkins has a digital number of 4, which is not promising. An ordinary sort of person with middle or lower-class mores, he is conventional in his outlooks on sex, money and politics. At heart he is a breadwinner, and not much more. With 4's you can usually bank on a good deal of repression, and Richard Jenkins, whose heart number is 8 and whose personality number is 5, is repression with a capital R. Tied down by something — environment, perhaps — he is extremely ambitious, anxious to 'get away from all this,' and fiercely determined to do so, sink or swim. His personality number indicates that he is a bit of a rake as well; reckless love 'em-and-leave-'em type, half ready to seduce the most attractive woman in the area and half (or more than half) ready for a fight should the chance remark occasion it.

But the 8 points to something in his future: tough-minded, determined if not exactly enlightened, he will either succeed or fail in a big way; one thing's for certain, he's not going to end his life in a mining town in Wales. A practical, if inordinately ambitious man, he will assess his good and bad points and trade matter-of-factly on his talents; he is far too much of a 4, an open-faced 'square', to ever forget his limitations and his essential honesty will plague him throughout life when he comes to consider his failings. But he is out to succeed, or drop deeper than did any plummet sound. The 5 in his personality number indicates impatience, sexual activity carried at times to extremes, nervousness, charm, and a quality which I can only self-contradictorily define as generous egotism. A sort of 'good guy' if you can get under his skin, but a most anxious and unfulfilled individual.

When Richard Jenkins becomes Richard Burton, his heart number (indicating his aspirations, secret wishes) becomes his digital number (indicating general state in life). This is often the case with people who change their names, as with Edward Alexander Crowley, who decided,

at maturity, to call himself Aleister. Richard Burton's digital number is 8, the number of great worldly success, or failure. He has become in fact what he has always been in secret; the adventurer, the speculator, the do-or-die businessman who will risk a million if the odds are proved, to his satisfaction to be right. His heart number becomes 6, which indicates that with all the worldliness, he has now acquired a taste for security, warmth, comfort, a home life of his own making. For all his early sexuality, he is still instinctively monogamous, the original carrier of the double standard, in fact. What he wants most now that he has attained his original ambitions is peace. But his ego, never a small commodity with 8s, has carried his personality number to 11, which his public image shares with the essential number of a Churchill. He is no longer a mining-town playboy; he and his followers see him as commensurate with Einstein (another 11) in influence and power, and as his 8-nature leads him to greater and greater success he will find privacy that much more difficult to attain. Immensely prosperous, but a homebody by birth, he is in a sense hoist on his own petard.

The intelligent reader will observe that I might have discovered all these aspects of the character of Richard Burton through nothing more occult than a close study of past files of popular newspapers. The perceptive will appreciate that I had to choose a public figure (I chose Burton at random) to make any sort of contact with my readers, and the curious will attempt an analysis with the name of someone neither he nor I have met before, or perhaps someone close to him, to see how the system works.

Left: *Richard Burton, whose original digital number was the inauspicious 4 when his surname was Jenkins, is now a number 8—the number of great worldly success or failure.*
Right: *Like a great many actors, Marlon Brando has the number 7—the number traditionally of mystery, secretiveness and discipline, though 7s are often bitter and sarcastic too.*

Fortune Telling With Numbers: The 'Pythagorean' System

This is a very old method of divination as given by Kozminsky, who tells us it is 'ascribed to Pythagoras and may be authentic'. It is certainly as effective a means of fortune-telling as any other not specifically invoking a deity or involving simple, unaided clairvoyance. I cannot impress upon the reader too strongly the importance of not regarding this or any other means of divining as a party game if he sincerely wishes to obtain results.

Take a clean sheet of paper and divide it into four squares. Into each square inscribe the following numbers.

I					II		
1	2	3	4	7	10	16	17
9	11	13	14		18	20	21
					24	26	27
5	6	8	12		22	25	28
15	19	23			29	30	
	III					IV	

SQUARE I foretells success in a short time. It indicates youthfulness. Its time is spring.
SQUARE II foretells a successful outcome, but indicates some annoyance and delay in the meantime. Tall, dark persons. Autumn.
SQUARE III is potentially unfortunate news; failure without delay. Summer. 'Short, fair people.' (*Kozminsky*).
SQUARE IV is unfavourable as well, but indicates that failure will be longer in coming. Winter. Short persons with dark colouring.

The numerological-literal equivalents are these:

2	3	4	6	8	9	11	12	13	16	18
Y	Z	A	B	Q	O	I	E	X	K	D
		F	T			U	J	L		W
		S				V	N	R		
							P			

19	21	26	28
M	G	C	H

In addition, you will need the following correspondences.

Moon	=	45	Sunday	=	106
Sun	=	34	Monday	=	52
Mercury	=	114	Tuesday	=	52
Venus	=	45	Wednesday	=	102
Mars	=	39	Thursday	=	31
Jupiter	=	78	Friday	=	68
Saturn	=	55	Saturday	=	45

The sun governs Sunday; the Moon, Monday; Mars, Tuesday; Mercury, Wednesday; Jupiter, Thursday; Venus, Friday; Saturn, Saturday.

Sit down before your square of paper, close your eyes, take a few deep breaths and clear your mind completely. Now gradually allow the question you wish answered to form itself in your mind; if it involves a situation, make as clear a pictorial image of the situation as you possibly can. If it involves another person, visualize him or her so strongly that you can smell his aftershave or her perfume. Now let a number from 1 to 30 spring into your mind. Pay close attention to your thoughts, and be sure and settle on the *first number* that occurs to you.
Now add the following:
    Number thought of
+Number of 1st letter of your 1st name
+Number of the day on which you are working
+Number of the planet governing that day
Divide the sum by 30 (the numbers in your square, by the way, as you may have noticed, range from 1 to 30). Discard the first sum, using *only the remainder*. This is the number to find in the appropriate section of your square, and it should give you your answer. If your question is concerning health, the moon's age must be added as well; this can be determined by the use of an almanac or by simply telephoning an observatory. Kozminsky lists also a number of days in each month during which this experiment should not be carried out; since today, January 5, is one of them, I shall close here.

Right: *The contemporary artist, Maggie Raynor's free representation of numbers used in the art of numerology. They are depicted as active and alive, tumbling out of boxes, almost as if they had a will of their own. This sense of the vitality of numbers is central to the whole concept of numerology.*

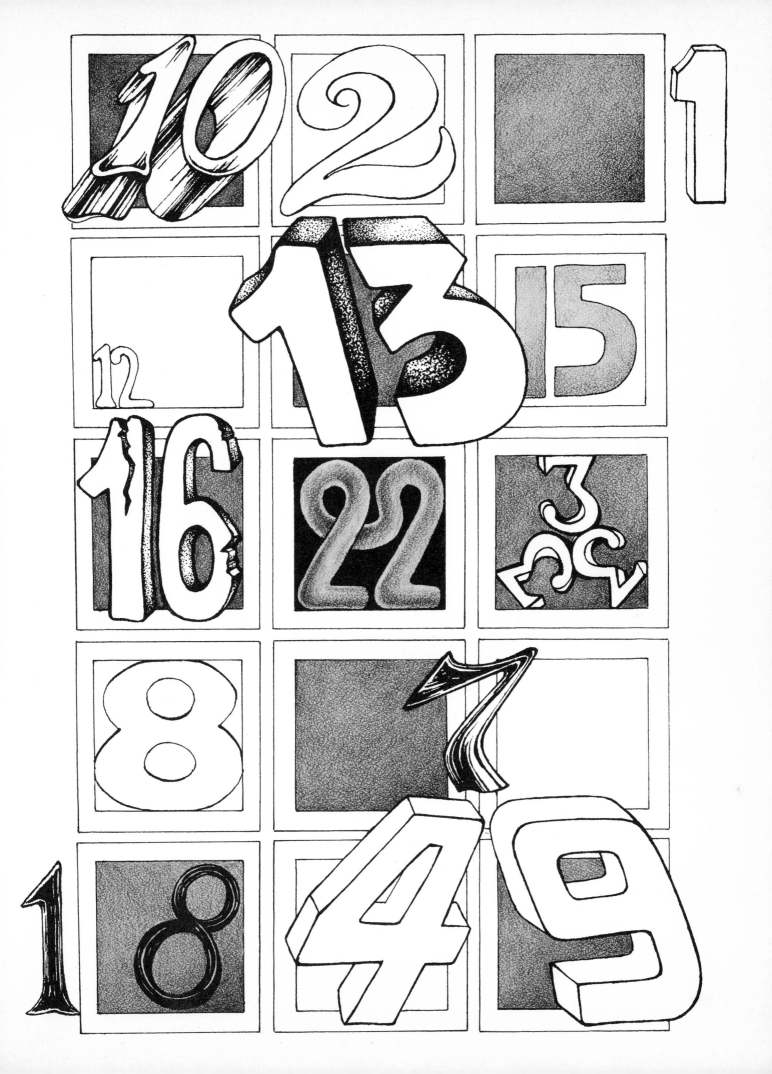

I CHING

The *I Ching* — a collection of magic spells; a do-it-yourself form of divination; totally unintelligible; a book of profound wisdom. These are some of the phrases that have been used to describe this most ancient Chinese book. Those who have found it useful have returned to its pages time and time again, while those who did not find the solution to their problem, or an answer they liked, have discarded it as a book of lies and nonsense.

To say that the Book of Changes is an acquired taste would not be entirely true, but at the same time, it seems to be a system one either likes or hates — a purely personal thing. Perhaps this is because the *I Ching* requires a little more effort than most other divination methods. The original method of consulting the oracle appears to be highly complex and difficult for the beginner, while the wording of the texts used to answer the questions is either rather elusive or downright obscure at times. Luckily, however, with a little patience and application, this form of divination becomes quite simple and extremely helpful when used correctly.

According to tradition, the *I Ching* dates back at least four thousand years, but there is also reason to believe that it is so ancient that its origins go far beyond historical memory. In any case, one thing is certain — it is a very old system and one of the world's oldest books. The first author is said to have been Fu Hsi, a legendary figure who was the first person to invent linear signs, whilst the present texts and commentaries are ascribed to King Wen and his son, the Duke of Chou. Confucius is also said to have been a contributor and it is said that he wished he could have lived another fifty years in order to complete his studies of the *I Ching* and

Left: *A porcelain figure of Li T'ieh Kuai, one of the eight immortals of Chinese mythology, portrayed as a beggar leaning on a crutch.*
Right: *A Chinese red lacquer panel decorated with symbols from the 'I Ching'.*

thereby perhaps have become a man without any grave faults.

Since the first English translation of the *I Ching* appeared during the late nineteenth century, its popularity in the West has slowly been spreading until now more and more people are eagerly consulting it for help with all their problems. It has particular appeal for young people of today who are aware enough to realise its potential, although more men seem to prefer it than women, which is a pity since a great deal more could be revealed through intuition, and women in general seem to be rather more receptive than men. The famous psychologist C. G. Jung spoke highly of the *I Ching* and regarded it as a "great and singular book". He even wrote the foreword to the translation (originally in German) by Richard Wilhelm showing that such was his belief in the system that he was not afraid to add his eminent name to the list of its devotees.

How and why does the *I Ching* work? What is it based on? Generally, the oracle works as an interpretation of polarity, that is the interaction between the opposites. The how and why of its mechanics can be explained in terms of the Jungian concept of syncronisity — a meaningful coincidence. The Chinese, like many other ancient peoples, conceived the universe as a dual principle. The first was male and was called Yang, being the embodiment of all that is positive, active, heavenly and light, etc. The second was Yin; the feminine principle containing all that is dark, earthy, negative and passive, etc. It is the movement of these two opposite but equal factors that has created the universe and keeps it in constant motion.

To represent these two conditions, the Chinese used symbolism, in their oracle. The Yang principle was portrayed as a single unbroken line (——) and the Yin principle as a broken line (— —). Broken lines are considered as yielding whilst unbroken ones are firm. Under certain circumstances, these lines become moving lines; the moving Yang being represented by the symbol ——O—— and the moving Yin by ——X——. This movement represents a state of fluctuation, whereby the Yang line will eventually change into a Yin line and vice-versa.

Originally, it would seem that the oracle was approached by using the Yang line as a "Yes" and a Yin line as a "No" but in time the lines were grouped together in pairs and then into threes and called trigrams. By combining the lines into groups of three the total number of symbols is eight and these eight trigrams are representative of all that happens in heaven and on earth. They are also in a state of continual change, one trigram changing into another throughout eternity. Therefore, these trigrams have been given names which are representative of certain aspects of nature. The eight basic trigrams are:—

—————— —————— ——————	CH'IEN	heaven, father, sky, creative, strong, active, firm, light, cold, etc.
— — —————— ——————	TUI	lake, marsh, rain, autumn, youngest daughter, joyful, pleasure, etc.
—————— — — ——————	LI	fire, lightning, sun, summer, middle daughter, beautiful, clinging, etc.
— — — — ——————	CHEN	thunder, spring, eldest son, activity, movement, arousing, etc.
—————— —————— — —	SUN	wind, wood, eldest daughter, gentle penetrating, etc.
— — —————— — —	K'AN	water, cloud, a pit, moon, winter, middle son, dangerous, enveloping, etc.
—————— — — — —	KEN	mountain, thunder, youngest son, stubborn, perverse, immovable, etc.
— — — — — —	K'UN	earth, heat, mother, receptive, responsible, passive, yielding, weak, dark, etc.

There are, of course, other meanings to the trigrams, but these are some of the basic ones. Others indicate certain animals and parts of the

Right: *Confucius, the great Chinese sage, is thought to have been a contributor to the 'I Ching'. It is said that he wished to live for another 50 years to complete his studies.*

body. As can be seen, there is also a family relationship between the trigrams of mother, father, youngest, middle and eldest son and youngest, middle and eldest daughter. These eight trigrams are further combined into sixty-four hexagrams, that is six-lined symbols consisting of two trigrams. It is the hexagrams that form the complete Oracle of Change.

Method of Divination—The Yarrow Sticks

The use of 50 yarrow sticks in working this oracle is the oldest method of divination by the *I Ching*. At first glance this is not an easy method but once mastered it really is easy, and is by far the best method. The reason for this is that the whole procedure is longer and more ritualistic, and gives the unconscious mind a greater opportunity to select the most appropriate hexagram. The more serious the approach to this type of divination, the greater the accuracy, and inci-

Left: *C. G. Jung, the famous psychologist, had a very high regard for the 'I Ching'.*
Above: *The Chinese traditionally used yarrow sticks to cast hexagrams.*

dentally, those who have consulted the oracle in a highly frivolous or disrespectful manner have quite often received a most rude reply.

Yarrow sticks can be obtained generally from shops which specialise in occult subjects. They come in packs of fifty. When not in use they should be kept in a piece of silk or other clean cloth and if possible stored in their own special box. Before using them you should always wash your hands so as not to contaminate the sticks with adverse vibrations and so spoil your answer. The wrapping cloth should be used to cover the working surface so that the sticks do not come into contact with the table that you are using. If you intend to study the *I Ching* seriously it is advisable to obtain a book of the actual translated texts or to copy them into a special little book. This should also be kept wrapped in silk when not in use and treated with the same respect as the yarrow sticks. The best book to get is the classic translation by Richard Wilhelm but there are others available which are more simplified versions, so choose the one which will suit your needs.

When consulting the oracle, a little incense should be burned to aid receptivity and according to tradition, the person using the oracle should face south. The sticks should be removed from their container and passed through the incense smoke three times in a clockwise manner with the right hand while concentrating on the question. Be sure that your question is precise and to the point, if it is vague, the answer will also be vague, if you get one at all. After this, replace one of the sticks in its receptacle so that that you only have 49 in hand. Divide the remaining sticks as equally as possible into two piles with the right hand and place one stick from the right pile between the ring and little fingers of the left hand. Separate four sticks from the left pile and then another four sticks and another, etc., until there are only one to four sticks left. Place these remaining sticks between the next two fingers of the left hand. Remove sticks from the right hand pile, four at a time until one to four sticks are remaining. These are placed between the next set of fingers.

The sticks in the left hand are now counted and the number of sticks should be either five or nine. If you have any other figure then something is wrong as these are the only two possible combinations of numbers — 1+1+3 or 1+2+2

or 1+4+4 or 1+3+1. The law of averages makes five the most numerous number to appear however. These sticks should then be placed to one side. The discarded sticks from the first procedure should then be put together and the process repeated. The number should now total either four or eight sticks — 1+1+2, 1+2+1, 1+3+4, 1+4+3. Place these to one side next to the first five or nine sticks. The remaining sticks are gathered together once more and the process repeated a third time. The total will be four or eight sticks held in the left hand, as above.

The three piles of sticks which were put to one side will now tell you whether the first line of the hexagram is a Yin, Yang or moving line. Incidentally, in building a hexagram they start at the bottom and work up, so that the first line is the foundation, so to speak, of the rest. With the three piles there are the following compilations of sticks — 5 or 9+4 or 8+4 or 8 and the brief table underneath, showing all the possibilities obtainable will describe just what sort of line it is:—

Left: *The month of May—cherry blossom time— 'I Ching' hexagrams correspond to the seasons.*
Below: *The Samurai often used the 'I Ching' to predict the result of battles.*

5+8+8 — a Yang line (———)
9+8+4 — a Yang line
9+4+8 — a Yang line
5+4+4 — a moving Yang line (—O—)
5+4+8 — a Yin line (— —)
5+8+4 — a Yin line
9+4+4 — a Yin line
9+8+8 — a moving Yin line (—X—)

There is another method of working out the lines from the numbers of sticks obtained, but this is a little more difficult. The same procedure is repeated until a figure consisting of six lines has been built up while bearing the question in mind as much as possible. If there are no moving lines in the hexagram then the next step is to consult the text belonging to that hexagram. This single text should supply the answer to the problem in question. If there are moving lines then a new hexagram should also be built by changing the moving lines into their ultimate opposites. For example:—

Both the original and the new hexagram should be taken into consideration when inter-

preting the answer. If you wish to study the *I Ching* in greater depth you will find that the specific moving lines also have to be considered individually, but at this stage, consultation of just the two hexagrams will be sufficient.

The Coin Oracle

This method is very much simpler than the original method and is just as effective, providing that it is performed correctly. With this method there is a great temptation to repeat the question over and over again until a satisfactory, rather than a correct result is obtained. This reflects immaturity, and will only give bad results. For this method three coins are all you need. Some experts specify that Chinese coins with holes should be used, but these are not always obtainable. You might try to obtain some coins made from silver since silver is a very receptive metal. Whatever coins you use, these should also be kept wrapped and in their own container if possible.

The coins are thrown in the air six times, and each throw gives an indication as to the type of line. With the Chinese coins, the inscribed side is usually the Yin and the reverse the Yang.

However, you can choose which side represents what if you wish. If two Yang coins and one Yin fall, then the line is a Yang; if two Yin coins and one Yang fall, then the line is a Yin; if three Yang coins fall, then it is a moving Yang line and if three Yin coins fall, then the line is a moving Yin. The sixty-four hexagrams are all numbered and the following table will help you to locate the number and the correct text easily once you have constructed your figure. Each hexagram has a basic meaning and is followed by a short summary. The meanings are by no means complete and are a guide which should be useful for day to day life. The actual text, as I have said can be very obscure and requires a lot of study, as Confucius knew. There is also an indication of the time of year and month which is symbolised by the hexagram which should prove useful for the purposes of time definition. Remember, that the better the question in terms of accuracy and precision, the better the answer.

Below: *A beautiful Chinese plate decorated with the Yin and Yang of the 'I Ching'.*
Right: *A location table to help you find the number and text of the figure you have made.*

LOCATION TABLE

UPPER → / LOWER ↓	CH'IEN	CHEN	K'AN	KEN	K'UN	SUN	LI	TUI
CH'IEN	1	34	5	26	11	9	14	43
CHEN	25	51	3	27	24	42	21	17
K'AN	6	40	29	4	7	59	64	47
KEN	33	62	39	52	15	53	56	31
K'UN	12	16	8	23	2	20	35	45
SUN	44	32	48	18	46	57	50	28
LI	13	55	63	22	36	37	30	49
TUI	10	54	60	41	19	61	38	58

THE HEXAGRAMS

1. CH'IEN — CREATIVITY
Success through creativity; signifies everything that is masculine, active and heavenly; there may be danger but it is easily overcome. Corresponds to the month of May.

2. K'UN — PASSIVITY
Success after difficulty; advantages will be gained through friends; determination is needed; signifies all that is feminine, earthy and passive. Corresponds to the month of November.

3. CHUN — DIFFICULT BEGINNINGS
Difficulty followed by success; consolidate present position; the birth that follows is not easy; not the time to start something new. Corresponds to the month of December.

4. MENG — IMMATURITY
Good luck! Have patience; do not correct the faults of your juniors too severely; give advice when asked, but do not be used. Corresponds to the month of January.

5. HSU — WAITING
Travel at this time will lead to success; now is the time to sit back and let the future take its natural course. Corresponds to the month of February.

6. SUNG — CONFLICT
A situation that cannot be resolved successfully, therefore it is advisable to give up the whole idea. Do not travel at this time. Corresponds to the month of March.

7. SHIH — THE ARMY
If the question does not concern a military matter, this hexagram means the battle of life. Progress with a difficult and even dangerous task will win you respect; rely on expert opinion. Corresponds to the month of April.

8. PI — UNITY
Co-ordination; administration; cooperation brings progress; consult the oracle further; seek help from one in authority. Corresponds to the month of April.

9. HSIAO CH'U — THE LESSER NOURISHER
Care of the young; things are running smoothly but it is not yet time to take further action; good luck and improved conditions in the future. Corresponds to April.

10. LU — TREADING
Conduct; the present situation could become dangerous so be cautious; despite all risks you are likely to succeed. Corresponds to the month of June.

11. T'AI — PEACE
Harmony and good fortune; present difficulties can be overcome; inner strength. Corresponds to the month of February.

12. P'I — STAGNATION
Obstruction; an ominous sign; disharmony and weakness; those in authority are without virtue, be careful or you may become like them. Corresponds to the month of August.

13. T'UNG JEN — UNIVERSAL BROTHERHOOD
Lovers; friends; accept the situation for what it is. Where relationships are concerned, if the woman is dominant at the present time it is because the natural creative process wishes it so. This is not the time to complain. Corresponds to July.

14. TAYU — GREAT POSSESSIONS
Cultural achievement; fantastic success; good triumphs over evil;

those who are able to discriminate between reality and illusion will always be successful. Corresponds to May.

15. CH'IEN — MODESTY
Modesty brings success; travel at this time is fortunate; only those things which add to the general good will be successful. Corresponds to December.

16. YU — ENTHUSIASM
If you are certain that the present action is the right one, then proceed before it is too late. Be calm, have peace of mind. Corresponds to March.

17. SUI — FOLLOWING
Accept only what you know to be right and you will be successful. Beware of ulterior motives. Have confidence and do not be led into what you are not sure of.

18. KU — DECAY
Ruined work. The end is only a new beginning. Now is the opportunity to advance your own ideas and plans. Corresponds to March.

19. LIN — APPROACH
Great success will follow if things are put right. However, eight months later that success is liable to change to failure. Corresponds to January.

20. KUAN — CONTEMPLATION
Take a long hard look at your life and decide whether you are following the right path. If the enquirer is female, it will be to her advantage to keep a secret watch on the situation, even if it is rather sneaky. Corresponds to September.

21. SHIH HO — GNAWING
Success in legal proceedings. You are not to blame for the present trouble. Separateness. Corresponds to October.

22. P'I — ELEGANCE
Chance good luck. There is a small advantage in having a particular goal or destination. A time for watching and learning. Corresponds to August.

23. PO — SEPARATING
A time to get rid of hindrances, even if they are people. There is no goal or destination that can be pursued successfully at this moment. The inferior are flourishing and you are in danger of losing. Corresponds to October.

24. FU — RETURN
Self-discipline and kindness to others is necessary. The willing acceptance of movement brings success provided there is a goal or destination in mind. Friends arriving. Corresponds to December.

25. WU WANG — THE UNEXPECTED
Integrity. Only those who do what is right can expect to succeed. Those without integrity will suffer. No point in having a goal at the moment. Corresponds to the month of September.

26. TA CH'U — THE GREAT NOURISHER
Entertain friends outside the house. A good time for travelling. Success only if you persevere with what is right. Corresponds to August.

27. I — NOURISHMENT
Consistent effort brings good success. Observe and learn from the habits and experiences of others. Corresponds to November.

28. TA KUO — EXCESS
Have a firm goal in mind to supplement any weakness in plans. Indi-

cates something too large or excessive in other ways. Corresponds to October.

29. K'AN — THE ABYSS
Great danger. Keep a tight rein on the mind to prevent illusion and fear. Be confident. Corresponds to the period from November to January.

30. LI — FIRE
Flaming beauty; dependence. Good fortune can be gained by looking after those who need help. Clear the mind and the way to success and good fortune will also be clear. Corresponds with the period of May to July.

31. HSIEN — INFLUENCE
Attraction and stimulation. Good fortune will result from taking a wife. Persistence brings rewards. Corresponds to May.

32. HENG — DURATION
The long enduring; that which will take a long time to complete. Success through perseverance and freedom from error. Corresponds to July.

33. TUN — RETREAT
Yielding. Persist only in small things and pay attention to detail. Not a time for great achievement. Corresponds to July.

34. TA CHUANG — THE POWER OF THE GREAT
Only the strong and persistent wield power. Time to get out of that nice comfortable rut. Corresponds to March.

35. CHIN — PROGRESS
Merit is rewarded. Some small assistance, probably from a woman. Do not push on blindly. Be generous, the good you can do for others will reflect on you.

36. MING I — DARKENING OF THE LIGHT
Steadfastness in the face of difficulty. Put aside selfish thoughts, but do not go to the other extreme. It may be wise to hide your light under a bushel for the moment. Corresponds to September.

37. CHIA JEN — THE FAMILY
Put family happiness above personal happiness. Everything to do with the household is well aspected. A good omen for women but not for men unless there is a moving line.

38. K'UEI — OPPOSITION
Estrangement. Do not be encouraged to do too much. Take pleasure in the small things. Trouble is not permanent and delay has its purpose. If a slight setback occurs, then it is a sign of sure success to come. Corresponds to December.

39. CHIEN — TROUBLE
Difficulty and perhaps even danger lies ahead, but do not take the seemingly easy and dishonest way out. Seek good advice from a person in authority or one of wisdom. Corresponds to November.

40. HSIEH — RELEASE
The west and south are favourable. Those with nothing to gain from present plans should give them up. Those with much to gain should speed things up if they are to be successful. This is not the time to stand still.

41. SUN — REDUCTION
Loss at first, but have confidence as success is ahead. Be adaptable and use things that come to hand easily. Not a good time for permanent actions such as marriage or business. Corresponds to July.

42. I — GAIN
There is nothing to stop progress. Good fortune, especially with any-

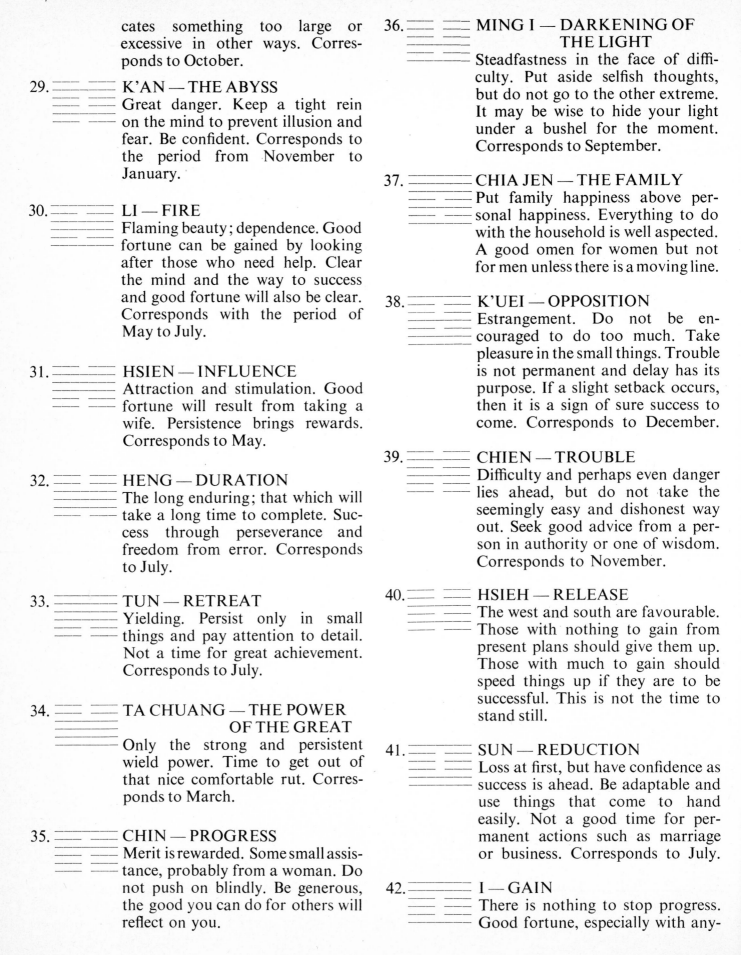

thing connected with wood. Past actions are now bringing benefits. It would be to your advantage to show your superiors your trustworthiness. Corresponds to the month of January.

43. KUAI — BREAKTHROUGH
Resolution. Do not take on difficult tasks through vanity. Frankness could be dangerous at the moment. Trust only those you are sure of. Corresponds to April.

44. KOU — CONTACT
All types of business and social contact, meetings, intercourse, etc. This is not a time to marry for men. If they do it is likely that the woman will be the boss. There is present difficulty that can be overcome by persistence and caution. Give to others what is their right. Corresponds to June.

45. TS'UI — GATHERING
Get together to sort things out. The time has come to make some sort of sacrifice. Corresponds to March.

46. SHENG — PROMOTION
Timing is important at the moment. Take things slowly for a while and unexpected good luck will help you. There is nothing like solid faith to sustain you at the present moment. Corresponds to December.

47. K'UN — EXHAUSTION
Weariness. Success in spite of great difficulty providing you can manage to keep going. For most people this is not a good omen as the trouble is mostly self-made. A time to save one's breath. Corresponds to September.

48. CHING — A WELL
Do only that which is practical. Failure is likely to be caused by missed opportunities. Corresponds to May.

49. KO — REVOLUTION
Renovation — perhaps of character or home, etc. If you cannot adapt to the present situation, then you must try to overcome it. Before there is any progress radical changes must be made. Your regret and uncertainty will vanish with your success.

50. TING — SACRIFICIAL URN
Obligations and duties should be fulfilled as gracefully as possible. More energy and money should be expended on your fellow man rather than objects or ceremonies. Prestige holidays, parties and other entertainments count as ceremony. Things that are wrong or undesirable under normal circumstances, at specific times become acceptable. A missed opportunity could cause trouble. Corresponds to June.

51. CHEN — THUNDER
A time of success and achievement, even if you are a little too impetuous. Powerful beneficial forces are in action now. Corresponds to October.

52. KEN — KEEPING STILL
There is a time for action and a time for rest — be sure you are doing the right thing. Meditation may be of help. Corresponds to the period of February to April.

53. CHIEN — GRADUAL PROGRESS
Constant but gradual movement is the best. For a woman, marriage now will be a success. Fulfilment of desires. Corresponds to January.

54. KUEI MEI — THE MARRYING MAIDEN
Usually an unfortunate omen. As far as a woman is concerned, it is better to be a mistress than single. Advancement at the moment

would be disastrous. Beware of pride. Corresponds to September.

55. FENG — ABUNDANCE

Abundance may be of good or bad. May indicate too much of a good thing. The tide of fortune or misfortune can always quickly change. Do not take advantage of the generosity of friends — a miser usually ends up alone. Corresponds to June.

56. LU — THE TRAVELLER

No loss in travelling. Small matters will be successful. Plan wisely to avoid trouble, but you may be the victim of another's carelessness. Corresponds to April.

57. SUN — WILLING SUBMISSION

A certain amount of success to those who adapt to circumstances. Have a definite aim in mind. Visit a great or wise man. Corresponds to August.

58. TUI — JOY

Success and happiness but be on the look-out in case the situation should change. Follow the course you know is right. Corresponds to the period of August to October.

59. HUAN — DISPERSING

Safety. Long distance travel is favourable. In times of trouble rely on moral and spiritual values. Success needs generosity. Corresponds to June.

60. CHIEH — LIMITATIONS

Recognise your own failings. If your present course is causing you anxiety or regret then change it. Corresponds to July.

61. CHUNG FU — INNER TRUTH

Inward confidence and sincerity. The path you are taking is the only one possible. Have courage, be persistent. Corresponds to the month of November.

62. HSIAO KUO — THE POWERFUL SMALL

The small get by. A time of small successes. Do not undertake anything of great importance now. Aim at that which is in easy reach. Corresponds to January.

63. CHI CHI — AFTER COMPLETION

Good fortune in the beginning but disorder at the end. Do not attempt too much at the moment. Persist as best you can. Corresponds to the month of October.

64. WEI CHI — BEFORE COMPLETION

The present situation has more than half way to go yet. Expect set-backs, wait to see what will happen, and avoid excess in anything. Keep plans flexible. Corresponds to November.

Above: *This delightful picture of young boys playing bare-foot in the snow is again related to the seasonal changes indicated in the 'I Ching' hexagrams.*

HOW TO READ HANDS

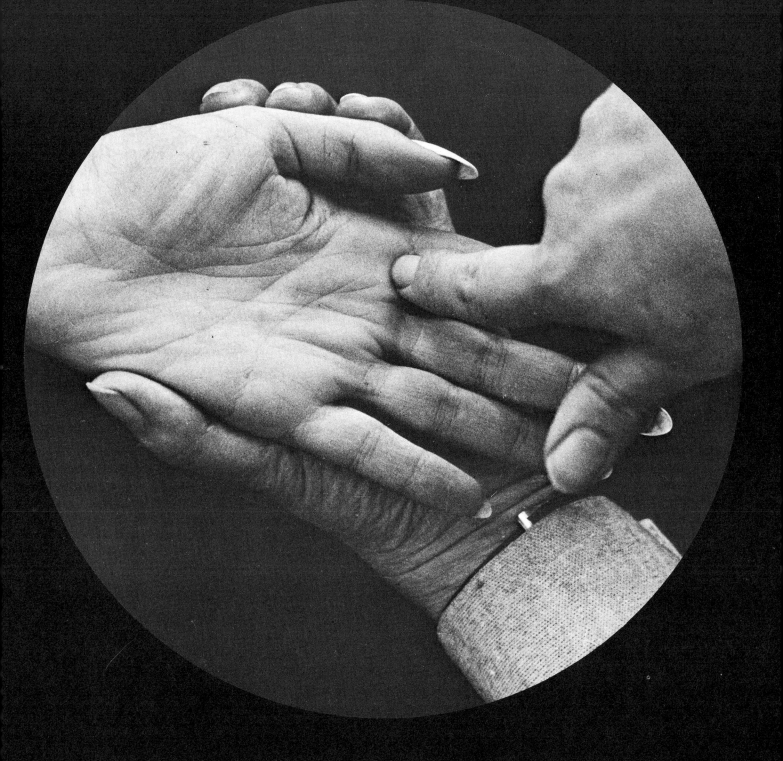

The lines and signs in your hands, so palmists have declared for centuries, are sure indications to your health, your character, your future and your fortune. If you are unhappy, feeling debilitated, worried about the bills, you may be able to conceal this by presenting a brave face to the world, but the lines and signs in your hands will reveal the true state of affairs. If you're content, full of health and vitality, solvent, in love, this shows in your face, and will also show clearly in your hands.

Psychologist Carl Jung made no secret of his conviction that the handprints and horoscopes of his patients gave him extra insight into their condition and future prospects. At this time few medical men were prepared to admit that they attached any value to the work of the seer. But now, as we come into the Age of Aquarius, things are changing. If you believe that the lines and markings in the hand have a meaning, you're now in very good company. There has been a massive probe into palmistry in England and the United States, and the conclusion reached is that the hands can indeed be helpful in diagnosing various physical, emotional and mental states. These conclusions did not amaze the palmists who had arrived at them many years earlier, but it's always pleasant to be proved right. And it does make it simpler for those who have always believed that there is something in palmistry to come right out and say so. Early in 1964 the *Lancet*, that sober British medical journal, published an article in which it was stated that handprints can be "a valuable tool" in diagnosis. In November of that same year, the United States Department of Health, Education and Welfare announced that they had enough evidence available to justify a research project, co-relating health indications with the lines and signs in palm and finger prints. Later, *Life* magazine published a splendidly illustrated feature entitled "Diagnostic Palmistry", giving a report on the work of two women doctors — Dr. Ruth Achs and Dr. Rita Harper — of New York's Downstate Medical Centre. Here the markings on a new born baby's hands are studied carefully, and have in certain cases alerted the doctors to hidden defects or ailments, which might otherwise have gone unnoticed.

Below: *This picture by Sir Joshua Reynolds is one of the many that have portrayed the art of palmistry.* **Right:** *The palm, showing the features used by the palmist to tell his subjects fortune.*

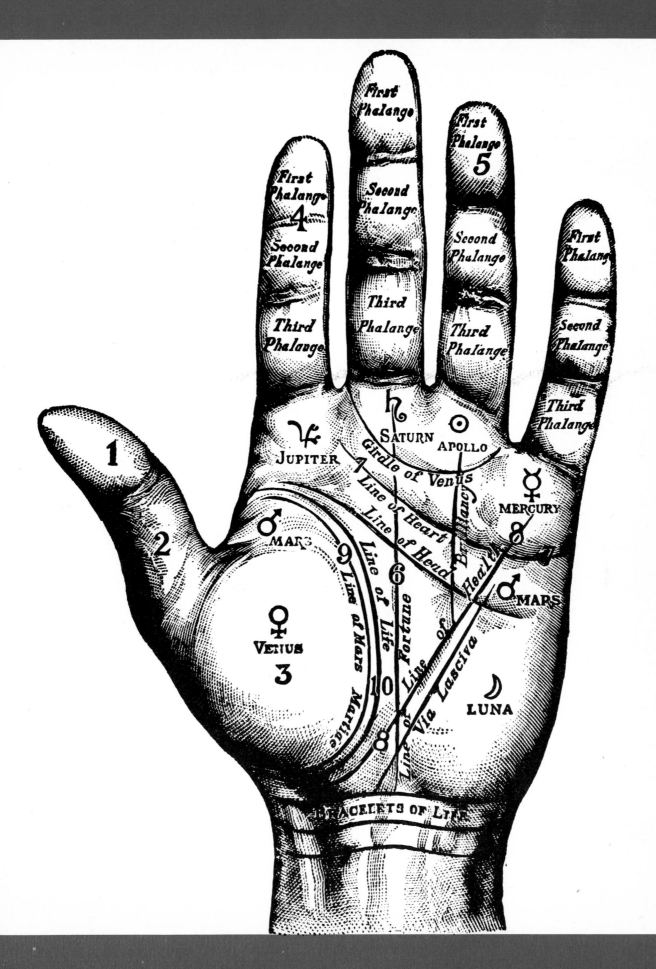

How to Read Hands

The easiest way to become an expert in this field is to study a hand you're really interested in — your own! Later, when you know more about it, you can astonish your friends by your uncanny skill. Don't be surprised if you find that your popularity zooms because people enjoy being told interesting things about themselves, and they're always eager to know what the future holds. You must, of course, be prepared to do your homework first, and memorise what the various shapes of the hand, and the signs on it, mean. It helps too, to take imprints of hands you know, and refer to them as you study.

How to Make Handprints

Place a writing or typing pad of thin, unlined paper on a flat, firm, surface. Ask the person who is having their hands read to take off any rings or jewellery and roll back their sleeves. Cover both palms, and the fingers and thumbs with a thin film of lipstick. Ask them to press one hand gently on the paper. Then ask them to lift the hand up from the paper, being careful not to smear the imprint. Repeat with the other hand. It's not quite as simple as it sounds, but after a few trials and a lot of patience, you'll manage the knack. Write the date of the reading on the imprint sheets. If, months or years later, you make another set of imprints of the same hands, you will almost certainly see some changes. The lines and signs in the hand do alter according to time and changing circumstances — only the patterns of the fingerprints remain the same.

Right or Left?

In giving a reading, it is always necessary to look at *both* hands. In a right-handed person, the left hand symbolises the subconscious, and tells you about the qualities the person is born with. The right hand symbolises the conscious mind, and tells you whether or not the inborn qualities have been developed, and to what extent. In a left-handed person, reverse these indications.

Chirognomy

Now we come to Chirognomy, which deals with the actual shape and size of the hand. Already you know that the lines and signs on the palm can yield many valuable clues to temperament and destiny. It may be news to you that shape and size of the hand can be revealing too.

Small Hands: The man whose hands are rather small in comparison with the rest of his build, thinks big. He quickly grasps the main points of a situation, and can map out a master plan rapidly; he does, however, prefer to leave the detailed work to others. He makes snap decisions and goes into action without any hesitation. He can sum up people at a glance, knows intuitively who can be trusted, and who is unreliable and likely to let him down.

Large Hands: The man whose hands are large in comparison with the rest of his build is thoughtful, reflective and analytical. Privacy is essential to him. There are times when he must be alone, to retire within himself, to think quietly about things, and re-charge his batteries. Never try to rush him into anything, never try to force any issues for he likes to take his time. He carefully weighs up all the pros and cons before he makes up his mind about anything. Large hands can indicate skill in fine, delicate work,

The Various Shapes of the Hand

Hands can be divided into four basic types so far as the shape is concerned.

The Square Hand: This is easy to recognise at a glance. The palm is as long as it is broad, and the finger-tips are rather square. The breadth of the palm indicates strength, tenacity, the desire and ability to work hard. Square-handers are level-headed, practical, conscientious, conventional. They like to build their lives on a solid foundation and are very security-conscious.

The Psychic Hand: Almond-shaped nails, a narrow palm, tapering fingers are the special characteristics of psychic-handed people. It's hard to judge them by ordinary standards; they're highly sensitive, with intuitive gifts which enable them to pierce the veil of the future, and to know things ahead of time. Fatalistic, idealistic and emotional, they generally need someone shrewd and sensible to look after them.

Right: *A great deal can be learned from looking at the shape of a particular hand. The four main shapes are the square, the spatulate, the artistic and the psychic, as shown in the diagrams.*

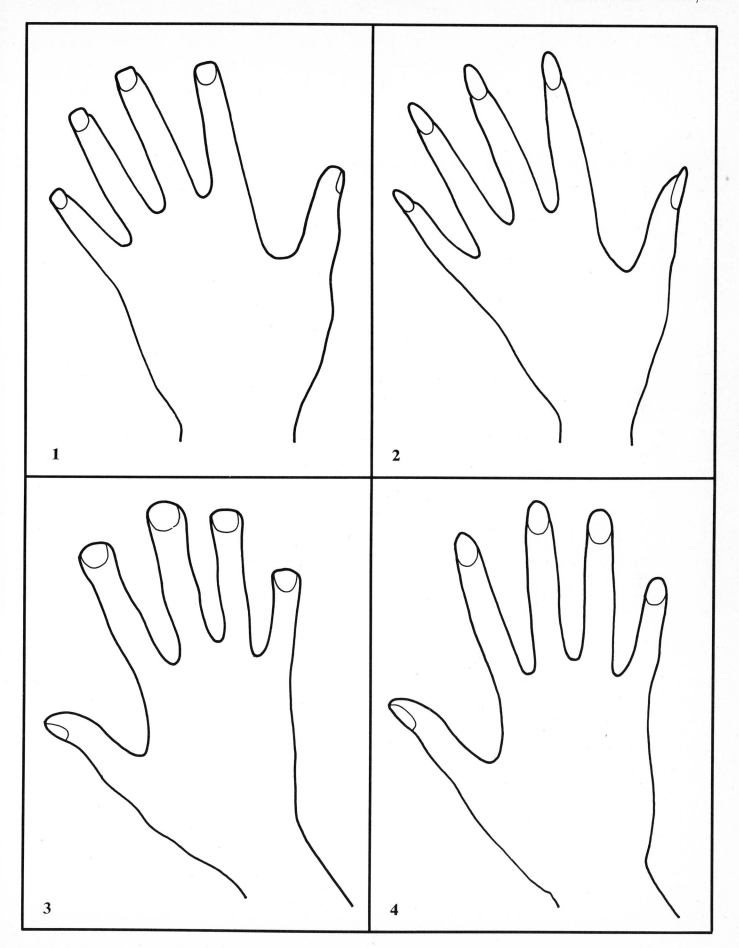

The Spatulate Hand: Look at the fingers, and you'll find that they resemble a chemist's spatula, widening out at the finger-tips. If you can stand the pace, these people are wonderful to be with — stimulating, self-confident, energetic and resourceful. They are the eternal seekers, dissatisfied with a routine existence. Original and inventive, they are always eager to explore new paths and new ways of thinking.

The Artistic Hand: Again we look at the fingers and observe that they are wide at the base, and narrow gradually to rounded finger-tips. There's a strongly creative inclination here, which finds an outlet whenever possible in the arts — writing, music, painting — or in the world of entertainment. Artistic-handed people are imaginative, impulsive, unconventional. They prefer an occupation which gives them a sense of satisfaction, even if it's poorly paid.

Palmistry Proper

In palmistry proper, the important lines are the Life-line which surrounds the base of the thumb. The Head-line, which runs across the middle of the palm. The Heart-line, which you will see just under the finger-bases. The Line of Fate which runs upwards from the wrist to the base of the second finger, and the Line of Sun — the companion line to the Fate-line — which ends under the ring or Sun finger.

The Life-line: Look at Fig. 5 and you will see that the Life-line embraces the fleshy pad at the root of the thumb which is called the Mount of Venus. When the Life-line is generously curved, and comes right down to the wrist without any breaks, this indicates a sound constitution, long life and vitality. That generous curve also shows emotional warmth, cheerfulness and generosity. A shorter Life-line with a less generous curve shows a less robust constitution, and a cooler, more self-contained temperament and attitude to life. If the Life-line is short or broken, don't jump immediately to the conclusion that the life-span will be short. Examine the thumb. If it is strong, and has a long well-shaped nail section, this indicates strong will-power; the owner will hold onto life with dogged determination. Sometimes another, finer, quite separate line can be seen inside the Line of Life. This is called the Inner Life-line or the Line of Mars (Fig. 6) and

reveals powerful inner forces and strength which support the owner in times of danger or illness. It also suggests a fondness for physical pleasures and the drive and ability to gain a high position in life.

The Source of the Life-Line

Where does the Life-line begin? The point where it starts gives a valuable clue to temperament and destiny. Usually it starts under the Mount of Jupiter, which is the little raised pad at the base of the index or Jupiter finger. Sometimes, however, you will come across a Life-line which begins higher up, on the Mount of Jupiter itself. (Fig. 7). This means that the owner is ambitious, and forecasts success, rewards and recognition. A Life-line with the usual starting-point, which has a branch-line running up to the Mount of Jupiter has much the same significance — it points to a self-confident, ambitious temperament, and is an omen of success. (Fig. 8). A branch-line from the Life-line to the Mount of Saturn (Fig. 9) represents struggle — nothing comes easy. Hard work and patience will be required if success is to be gained. A branch-line running up from the Life-line to the Mount of Sun (Fig. 10), the raised pad of flesh at the base of the ring finger, predicts that the owner's special skills and talents will be recognised and rewarded. This "branch-line to fame" is often seen in the hands of people in the public eye such as actors, singers and artists.

The Life-line which ends in a fork (Fig. 11), with one prong curving across the hand to the Mount of the Moon, indicates overseas travel. Palmists call this fork the Sign of Two Flags. People with this sign have the wander-lust; they travel far, and spend some part of their life in a foreign country. The Life-line which begins by just touching the Head-line shows good sense, prudence and moderation. (Fig. 12). When the Life-line is closely connected or "tied" to the Head-line, this suggests that the owner lacks confidence, is inclined to be over-cautious and finds it hard to make decisions. Such people are easily wounded by criticism, but praise and appreciation work wonders for them. (Fig. 13).

Right: *The life line is of great interest to the palm reader, who examines not only the length of the line, but also the various sources on the hand.*

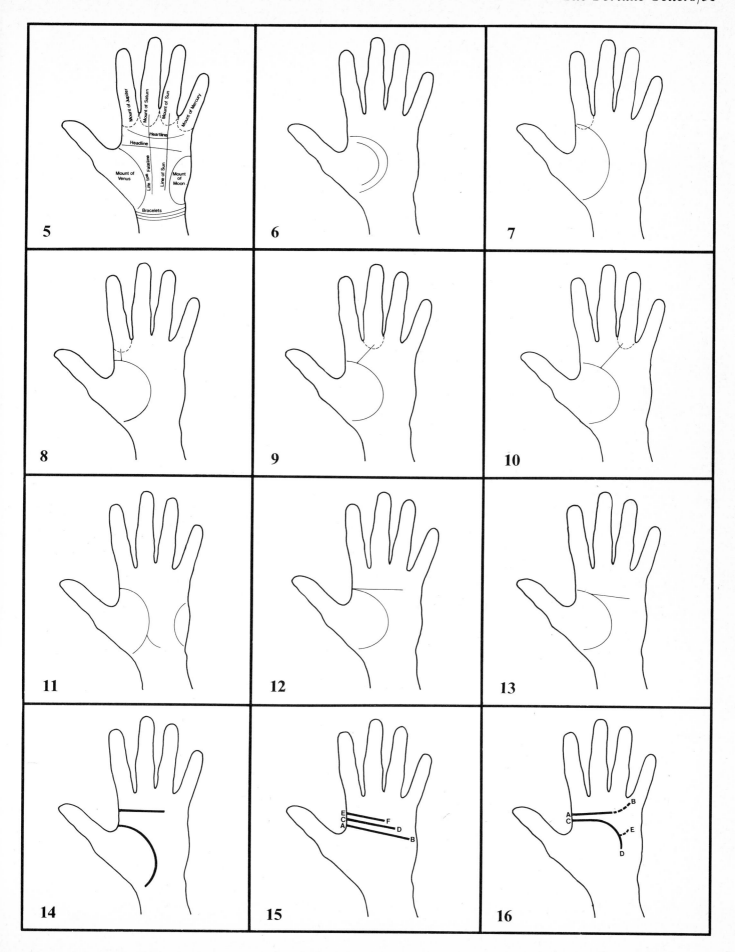

A wide space between the Life-line and the Head-line shows over-confidence and courage that amounts to recklessness. (Fig. 14).

The Head-Line

The *length* of the Head-line reveals intelligence — or the lack of it. The *direction* which the Head-line takes is a useful pointer to the kind of intelligence the owner is endowed with, and in which areas it is likely to operate. The owner of a Head-line which is so long that it reaches almost to the edge of the palm farthest from the thumb has an exceptional mind; he is in the genius bracket, (Fig. 15, AB). Average intelligence is denoted by the Head-line which runs about three-quarters way across the palm. (Fig. 15,CD). The short Head-line, terminating half-way across the palm, is an indication of mental instability, weak will-power and a very low I.Q. (Fig. 15,EF). The Head-line which runs straight across the palm points to a logical, down-to-earth, practical mind. (Fig. 16,A). When the Head-line is for the most part straight, but curves upwards at its end towards the Mount of Mercury under the little finger, this suggests the Midas touch — everything the owner handles turns to gold. (Fig. 16,AB). The Head-line which slopes gently downwards shows a gentle, idealistic temperament; intuition, imagination, a gift for music or acting, a talent with pen or brush. (Fig. 16,CD). When this Head-line terminates in a fork, versatility and adaptability are indicated. When one prong of the fork points upwards towards the Mount of Mercury, this is a promise that the owner's creative talents will be handsomely rewarded. (Fig. 16,CDE). Too narrow a space between the Head-line and the Heart-line is not good; it means that the heart rules the head.

The Heart-Line

According to the popular song: "Love and marriage, love and marriage, go together like a horse and carriage". Sometimes they do and sometimes they don't, but it is undoubtedly a fact that many of the questions put to the palmist connected with these two important areas of the life. Let us discover a few of the answers by examining the Heart-line which runs across the palm at the base of the fingers.

Compare it first of all with the Head-line. When the Heart-line looks longer and stronger than the Head-line, this is an indication that the owner is motivated more by emotion than by logic. When the Heart-line takes second place to the Head-line we may then conclude that reason rules, and dominates the feelings. The person concerned has a practical outlook on life and the emotions are kept firmly in check. The Heart-line which runs right across the palm shows an excess of affection and possessiveness which too often results in misery. (Fig. 17). Given sound advice, such people may make an effort to be more trusting, less demanding, and thus save themselves and those connected with them a load of unnecessary grief and trouble.

The Heart-line which begins on the middle of the Mount of Jupiter — the little raised pad of flesh at the base of the index finger — hints that ambition will play an influential role in the love affairs and alliances of the owner. A man with this kind of Heart-line is selective; he wants a mistress or wife who will be an asset to him. A woman with this kind of Heart-line seeks a mate who is successful by worldly standards, and a good provider. (Fig. 18). The Heart-line which begins *between* the index and second finger is characteristic of the person who is not overly demonstrative, but who is, nevertheless, capable of staunch affection and loyalty. (Fig. 19). The Heart-line which begins with a small fork on the Mount of Jupiter spells luck and happiness in love. People who are blessed with this "fortunate fork" have the gift of sweet contentment, and their emotional relationships run smoothly as a rule. (Fig. 20).

However, when the Heart-line starts with a large fork, one branch on the Jupiter Mount and the other on the Mount of Saturn (the little raised pad of flesh at the base of the second finger), the portents are not so encouraging. Such people can be hot or cold, selfish or generous, serious or cheerful as the mood takes them. Unless they succeed in finding a partner who is endlessly patient and placid, their lives are liable to be riddled by complications and upsets. (Fig. 21). When the Heart-line begins on the Mount of Saturn itself, and is rather straight, a cool, self-contained disposition is shown. People in this group are worldly-wise and calcu-

Right: *People who are concerned about the pattern of their emotional lives are usually curious to know the traits revealed by their heart line.*

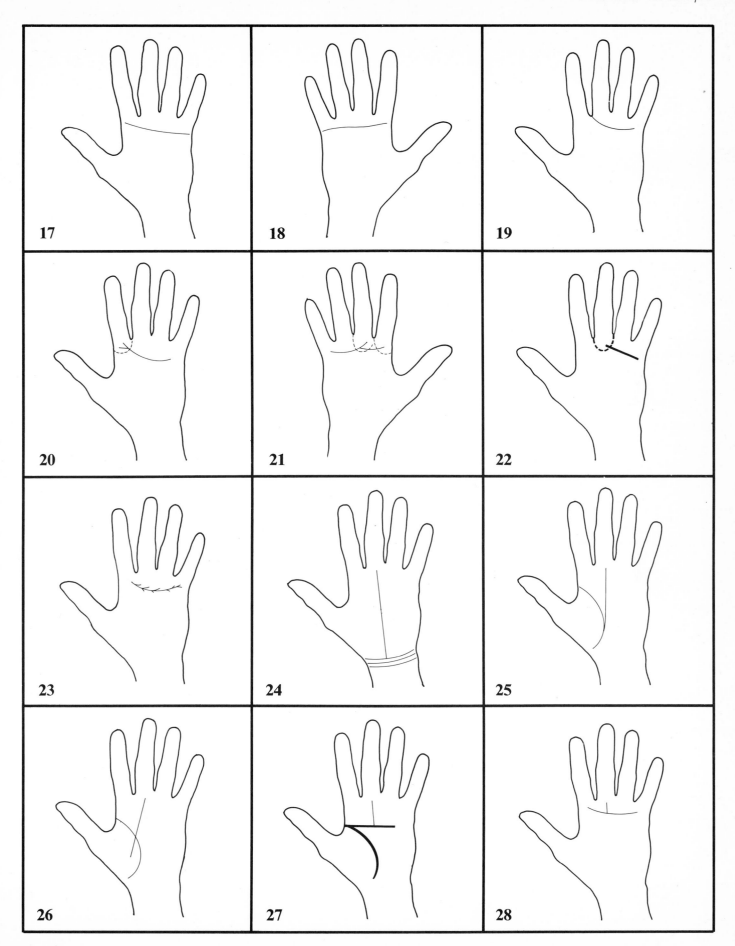

lating. They are seldom washed up lamenting on the wilder shores of love. (Fig. 22). The Heart-line with many fine little lines stemming from it, known as the Branched Heart-line, indicates a restless, seeking, flirtatious bent. These people butterfly from one affair to another before they finally settle down. (Fig. 23).

The Fate-Line

Palm-upwards, look at your wrist, and you will see, running across it, three lines which in palmistry are known as the bracelets. Regard the line nearest the palm as the top bracelet. When the Fate-line begins from the top bracelet, and runs up the palm to the Mount of Saturn at the base of the second finger, this forecasts early responsibilities. Unbroken and unmarred by adverse signs, it predicts good fortune and success. This type of Fate-line, which is rare, leads the owner straight to the pot of gold at the end of the rainbow. (Fig. 24).

The Fate-line, from any starting point in the hand, which runs up through the Mount of Saturn, and into the second finger, warns of failure, due to carrying things to excess. The Fate-line which starts from the Life-line declares that the early years have not been easy. The owner may have been held back and hampered in childhood. Progress tends to have been delayed by family duties and responsibilities. The point on the Life-line from which the Fate-line springs symbolises the moment when the owner is released from restrictions, free to forge ahead. (Fig. 25).

The Fate-line which starts from *inside* the Life-line, from the Mount of Venus, signals a much pleasanter, easier destiny — a happy, sheltered childhood, with love, help and encouragement in abundance; followed later by substantial aid from family sources to give the person concerned a good start in life. People with this kind of Fate-line are attached by strong bonds of affection and loyalty to the family, which may keep them from leaving home until rather late in life. Rather than strike out for

Below: *The main indicator of success and good fortune in life is shown by the line of the Sun. It can even reveal at what time in life success will come.*

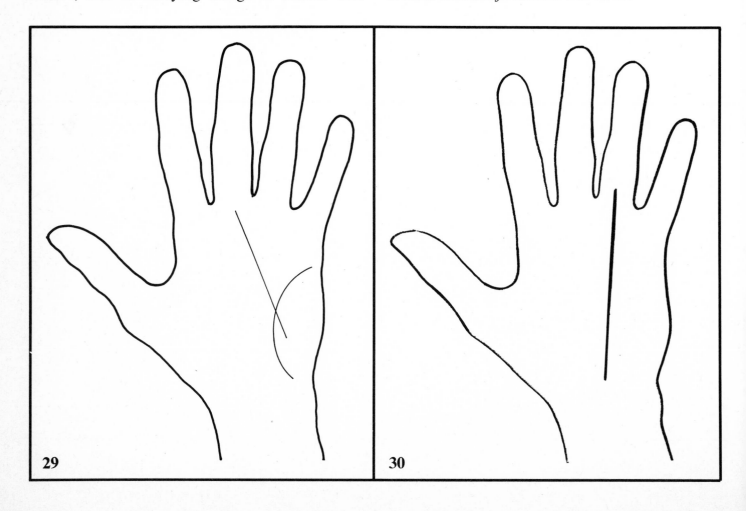

29   30

themselves and explore strange territory, they prefer to follow a family business or profession. (Fig. 26).

The Fate-line which springs from the Head-line points to hard work and struggle until success is won around the age of 35. Such people at least have the satisfaction of knowing that they have made it on their own merits, by using their intelligence. (Fig. 27). The Fate-line which starts from the Heart-line forecasts that the mid-fifties will be crowned by success. The autumn of the life will be secure and comfortable. (Fig. 28). The Fate-line which starts from the Mount of the Moon is frequently seen in the hands of gifted folk who have the power to influence the minds and emotions of the masses — politicians, lecturers, writers, actors, singers and artists. The opposite sex plays an influential role in their lives. They find it hard to settle in one spot, will travel far. Strangers bring them more luck than relatives. (Fig. 29).

The Line of Sun

The Line of Sun is one I am always delighted to see for it symbolises sunshine, success and triumphs. The person whose hand lacks this vital line may have all kinds of excellent qualities, but the life will be lived in obscurity; effort and merit go unrecognised and unrewarded. Starting from the wrist and proceeding unbroken and unmarred to the Mount of Sun, under the ring or Sun finger, its true termination, it symbolises a life of idyllic happiness and good fortune. This Line of Sun is usually seen only in the pages of palmistry text-books. (Fig. 30).

The Line of Sun which starts in the Life-line is a forecast of success, recognition and rewards for the owner's personal qualities and assets. Springing up from the Head-line, this is a happy prediction that the owner's skills and talents will be triumphantly rewarded and acclaimed. Springing up from the Heart-line, the Line of Sun suggests that the owner may have to wait for his — or her — ship to come in, but it will be well worth waiting for. This starting point of the Line of Sun signifies, for some, a late but happy marriage; and for all, security and contentment in retirement. The Line of Sun which begins on the Mount of the Moon predicts a golden future. It is seen in the hands of celebrities who rise to fame with the help of good fortune and the good-will of powerful allies.

The Thumb and Fingers

Having examined the various shapes of the hands, and the main lines on the palm, let's now take a look at the thumb and fingers, and find out what

Below: *The reading of palms enjoyed great popularity with the European nobility of the eighteenth century. To many of them it was a form of entertainment.*

they have to say about their owner's character and destiny.

The Thumb: Short-thumbed people are impressionable, impulsive, changeable in their ideas and attitudes, governed to a great extent by their emotions. A long, strong, shapely thumb shows the born leader, the person who is destined to get to the top. Such people think clearly, in a logical fashion. They have excellent powers of concentration, loads of determination and common sense. The unusually long, strong thumb holds a warning that its owner is a bossy, domineering, ruthless character who cares nothing for other people's feelings, and will, if necessary, ride roughshod over others to achieve his — or her — ends.

Stiff, straight thumbs betray a stubborn, reserved temperament. Their owners are inclined to resist anything new or experimental. They believe in disciplining their emotions; are slow and extremely cautious when it comes to making friends. However, when an attachment or alliance has been formed, they are completely dependable and loyal. Bendable, supple-jointed thumbs reveal an adaptable, tolerant, warm-hearted disposition. Such people spend money lavishly — when they have it — on whatever they fancy, and give generously when asked for help. They can move about from place to place without feeling uprooted, and enjoy meeting new people. Some may possess artistic or dramatic gifts.

The actual outline of the thumb can tell you if the owner is diplomatic, blunt or potentially violent. With the thumb-nail facing you, check if the thumb is approximately the same width from the root to the tip of the nail. It is? Then you may conclude that the owner is straightforward, forceful, direct, and sometimes too candid for comfort. However, you know where you stand with such an individual, which can be a help in these uncertain times. When the thumb narrows at the middle so as to give the impression of a "waist", a sharply contrasting character is indicated. The "waisted" thumb belongs to the intelligent, studious, tactful person, who is an adept at pouring oil on troubled waters, and bringing together those who have parted on bad terms. Such people fear to hurt others by giving their unvarnished opinion, and prefer to remain silent, or to wrap their thoughts in such discreet language that the listener sometimes imagines that they are being deliberately evasive. The short, broad, thick thumb, which in profile has the shape of a club, warns you that the owner has a violent temper, and will very likely resort to brute force if upset.

The Fingers

By now you know that each mount in the hand is ruled by one of the planets, and the same applies to the fingers. The first, or index finger is called the Jupiter finger. The second is called the Saturn finger; the third or ring finger is called the Sun finger, and the fourth or little finger is called the Mercury finger. The length, outline and flexibility or otherwise of the fingers can yield valuable information regarding the temperament and life-pattern. Short-fingered folk are active and intuitive. Long-fingered people are more reflective, more subtle, more concerned about detail, thinkers rather than doers.

In some hands the outline of the fingers is smooth and even. In others, large joints give them what palmists call a "knotted" look. Smooth-fingered people rely on flashes of insight rather than on logic; they base their conclusions and decisions on feelings rather than facts. They act first, without counting the cost, and think later. Knotted fingers belong to thoughtful, philosophical people who edit their words before uttering them, and have little time or inclination for small talk. Their detachment, dignity and values set them somewhat apart from the consumer society. They rate privacy, peace of mind and contentment higher than worldly renown and material possessions. Stiffly held fingers point to a rather cautious, rigid, set mentality. People with fingers like these will wait for a formal introduction before they speak to a stranger. When the stiffly held fingers are bent slightly inwards, this points to acquisitive tendencies. A request for a loan will be met with a dusty answer unless it's confirmed in writing that it will be returned by a definite date, with interest. Supple-fingered people have a large bump of curiosity or an inquiring mind, however you care to put it. Status, possessions, security are unimportant to them. When these supple

Right: *Palmistry has a very long history. This is a symbolic Roman hand cast in bronze, and showing zodiacal signs which because of their associations with planets are significant to palmists.*

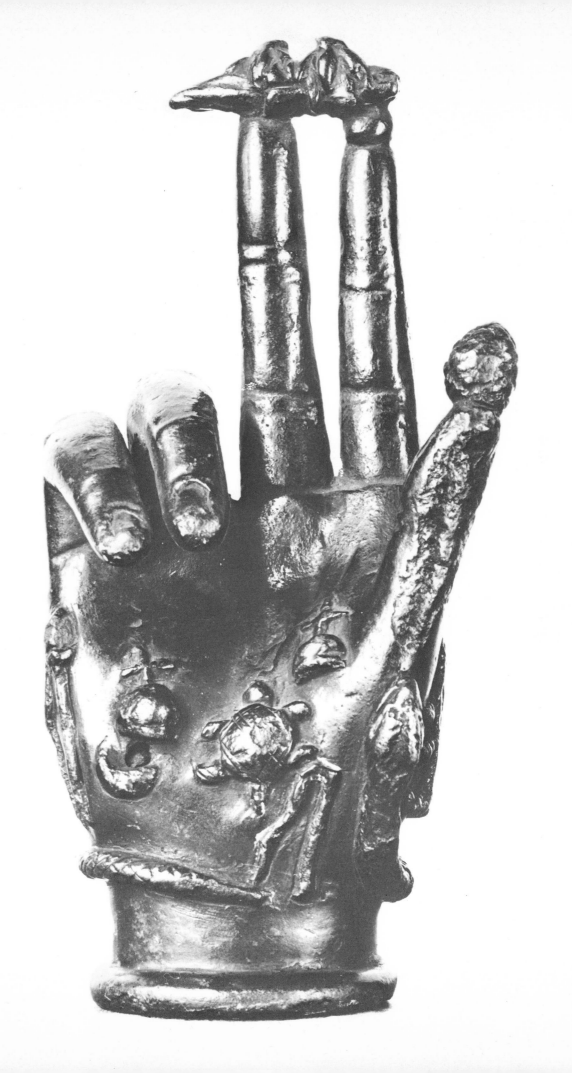

fingers are bent slightly backwards, this speaks of generosity to the point of recklessness. Such people are very warm, out-going, hospitable and good company.

The Index or Jupiter Finger

The length of each finger tells its own story. Begin by comparing the length of the index or Jupiter finger with the length of the ring or Sun finger. If they are equal in length, this is an encouraging omen. It is seen in the hands of people who are essentially reasonable, well-balanced, level-headed and quietly self-confident. They regard marriage as a partnership in which the man and woman have equal shares, and an equal say. The Jupiter finger which is shorter than the Sun finger is found in the hands of people who have a tendency to under-rate themselves. Modest, shy, rather retiring, they need lots of encouragement and reassurance. Heavy responsibilities frighten them, and they would rather take orders than give them.

The long Jupiter finger, by which I mean the index finger which is longer than the ring finger, announces that its owner is a born leader, capable and indeed intent on playing the masterful role. Such people, sometimes quite unintentionally, tend to overshadow weaker mortals by their high-powered personalities. When they are making a point, or giving orders — which happens a lot — they have a habit of wagging that long Jupiter finger in the other person's face in a very authoritative fashion. The Jupiter finger which is longer than the second or Saturn finger is the sign of the dictator.

The Second or Saturn Finger

When the second or Saturn finger is straight and in fair proportion to the other fingers, this indicates intelligence, good sense, a reasonable amount of caution, and the ability to study, concentrate and formulate long-term plans. However, a Saturn finger which is long and heavy so that it appears to dominate the hand, reveals an introspective, sober, sometimes pessimistic temperament. Saturn is described as the "stern task-master of the planets", and people with this kind of Saturn finger usually have a hard struggle to endure before they reach their goals. They get their education in the school of hard

knocks, and usually have to suffer privation, restrictions and loneliness before they win through to happiness. They are extremely self-disciplined, responsible and hard-working. Not the most light-hearted of companions, perhaps, but essentially realistic, down-to-earth and dependable.

The Ring or Sun Finger

As I have said earlier on, the Ring or Sun finger which is equal in length to the Jupiter finger reveals a well-balanced personality; someone who never goes to extremes. An example to us all. You will sometimes see a Sun finger which seems to bend towards, or lean a little on the Saturn finger. This indicates that the instinct of self-preservation is very strong indeed. Before making any decisions the owner will always want to know: "Will it pay me to do this?" When the answer is: "No," then he — or she — doesn't do it.

The long Sun finger, with a finger-print which looks rather like a coiled rope (palmists call this the "whorled" finger-print), is a very fortunate portent. Such people are born lucky. They can take a gamble and come out the winner. They seem to have the golden gift of attracting rewards and recognition for themselves. Their charm, sunny disposition, confidence and talents find a natural outlet in show business, the arts, public relations, sports, advertising and selling. They are not domesticated; too many cosy evenings at home bore them. They want to be out where things are happening, and they like to have lots of people around them to give them the stimulation, admiration and variety they need.

The Little or Mercury Finger

A short Mercury finger is not a good omen. It warns that the owner will encounter many difficulties and setbacks throughout life. With a good, strong thumb and intelligent Head-line the outlook is not altogether bleak; the chances are that such people may eventually achieve their goals, after a long struggle. The Mercury finger which curves gently in a little towards the Sun finger shows shrewdness in business, a knack for making money, and a flair for influencing and managing other people. These tendencies are strengthened when the Head-line curves up at its termination towards the Mount of Mercury.

Be on guard, however, whenever you see a crooked Mercury finger. This is the sign of the silver-tongued con-man — of someone who is smooth, diplomatic but unscrupulous and dishonest in business and financial affairs. The long Mercury finger, which extends beyond the second joint of the Sun finger, is the mark of the spellbinder. This length points to a quick, lively mind. Such people are full of ideas. They're articulate, versatile, adaptable, and can turn their clever hands to anything. They succeed as writers, teachers and actors and are attracted to healing, commerce, politics and occultism.

A True Story

Here is a true story of how some knowledge of palmistry can help to make a dream of love come true. A young woman whose horoscope I had prepared arrived for her consultation bearing a fragrant bunch of Spring flowers. She was a stranger to me. "Oh, how beautiful they are," I exclaimed. "Please accept them as a tiny token of appreciation for what you've done for me," she smiled. "Thanks to you I'm no longer lonely. I'm getting married in a few weeks' time to a man I adore." "What did I do?" I asked.

"Well, I was at home, re-reading your book *What Your Hands Reveal* when the phone rang, and it was one of my girl-friends inviting me to a party that same night. When I got round to her flat I saw this marvellous man — I'd seen him around a few times before and thought he was dreamy. But he'd never noticed me. This time, I looked very carefully at his hands, without making it obvious what I was doing. Then I wandered over to him, and said casually: "Are you a writer?" He looked stunned, and said: "What makes you ask me that? I've always wanted to write, but I've kept it a secret — something I do behind locked doors in my spare time. But in fact my first novel has just been accepted, and it's being published in the autumn. How *did* you know? You must be a very magical lady." "All I'd done, of course, was observe that his little finger was unusually long, and I remembered what you'd written about this in your book. I didn't tell him how I knew — I just smiled mysteriously. And we took it from there." Later I received an invitation to the wedding, and today this young woman is the wife of a man who is well on his way to making his name as an internationally acclaimed author.

Shaking Hands

In a chapter of this length it's just not possible to explain what all the lines and signs in the hands mean, but I can finish by telling you of another very simple, sometimes pleasant method of character-analysis, and that is — shaking hands! The hand that feels soft and plump when you shake it bears a message that its owner is addicted to the comforts and good things of life. These include love-making and not too strenuous leisure-time pursuits. The hand that feels dry, hard and stiff betrays a tense, inflexible, highly-strung temperament. The owner worries a lot, sometimes without good cause, and finds it hard to relax. The hand that feels firm but yet elastic to the touch is lucky. This person is cheerful, optimistic, positive, energetic, enjoying a sound constitution and excellent health.

Below: *This is a palmist's drawing of the left hand of the Empress Josephine. Drawn in 1827 it shows a long lifeline as well as pronounced lines for the heart and head.*

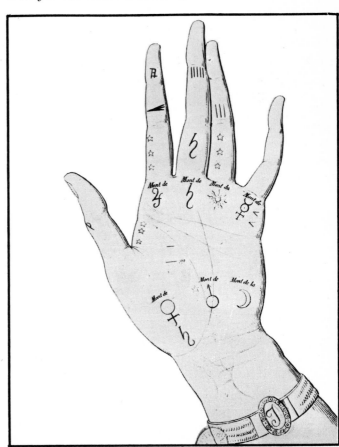

❧ THE RUNES ❧

Amongst the many forms of divination used in this modern world the runes are one of the least encountered and, as a consequence, many mysteries have gathered around them. But we "moderns" are not alone in our attitude towards this very ancient form of magic for even in the distant past, when runic lore was in vogue, they sustained an air of complete mystery. So let us see if we can unravel the skeins of this complex system by employing all that is available in scholarship and psychism in our quest.

The name rune comes from the German word *raunen*, which itself has several meanings. One translator states that it comes from the old Low German word which means to cut or carve, and thus the runes in ancient times were invariably cut or carved and not written. But another school of thought insists that the word means mystery or secret, so we are left with a choice. Latterly, raunen or rune came to designate the characters themselves so let us take it from there. Runes were by no means limited to the German races for they were venerated in Scandinavia generally and throughout the Anglo-Saxon world. The word "run" appears both in the old Anglo-Saxon and Icelandic languages, having the same magical connotations in each case.

Women Guardians

The magic of the Teutons was non heirophantic, and not in any way the province of a specialised priesthood, as was the case with the Celtic Druids, although both schools employed runic magic in their ceremonies. Amongst the early Teutons, women were the chief conservators of runic lore, but there was a very good and practical reason for this. The Nordic mysteries resided principally in the study and elucidation of the runic scripts just as in early Egypt it was part and parcel of the ability to decipher the hieroglyphic characters. Therefore, only those who could read the runes — or could read at all for that matter — were able to undertake a study of the occult. The unlettered warrior, too restless to apply his mind to the long study involved, made no progress in occult matters and had to rely on the womenfolk for his guidance.

Opposite: *The Yggdrasil, or Tree of Life, in the Norse tradition this fabulous tree was said to stretch from the highest heavens to the lowest depths of hell, encompassing the universe.*

Comparatively few were able to decipher the runes, even in olden times, so, in addition to the few ladies involved, the class of runic leaders was limited to leisured or wealthy people and lawmen. This power to decipher the unknown made such people a focus for mysterious veneration amongst the ignorant, and led to a belief that the ability to elucidate runes indicated the possession of super-human magical powers. Naturally the possessors made no effort to minimise this so the belief in their powers flourished. On the other hand, a certain amount of patience and natural ability were necessary to the acquirement of such an intricate script, so perhaps these magicians were in this way deserving of their veneration!

Not Just an Alphabet

Professor R. W. V. Elliot writes: "Communication among people remained a secondary function of runic writing throughout its long history, much more common was the use of runes to invoke higher powers to affect and influence the lives and fortunes of men." This was certainly true in earlier times, although later the word "runes" came to mean all alphabetical systems employed by the Teutonic peoples before the advent of Christianity. Where did the runes originate? Nobody knows to this day. Scholars have suggested hypotheses but the mystery remains unsolved. However, we can give a few of the ideas which have come to the fore from both academic and psychic sources.

Origins of the Runes

Some scholars say they are not Teutonic at all but are purely a transformation and adaptation of the Greek characters, whereas other authorities state that they have a Phoenician or even cuneiform ancestry. That they are non-Teutonic in origin is highly possible, apparently, as may be evidenced from their strong resemblance to other scripts. So the Teutons may have picked them up from a much earlier and more sophisticated civilisation, which leaves us with hints of Atlantis and the like. But this is pure speculation so let us content ourselves with what we have by way of evidence today.

Runes have been divided into three systems — English, German and Scandinavian — but the difference is purely local As I have already said, they were not employed for literary purposes in early times, and therefore wherever their inscriptions are found there is some magical meaning behind them Archaeology shows that they were generously inscribed on stone monuments, implements of all kinds, weapons and personal ornaments and furniture. They are to be found in all places where those great adventurers, the Vikings, set their feet and in England, for example, they are frequently encountered in the north where the Scandinavian influence was the strongest.

Symbolic Sounds

The first letters of the runic alphabet have the powers of the letters f, u, th, o, r, c, for which reason the order of the runic letters is called not an alphabet but a FUTHORC or FUPARK, the "p" equalling "th". The system is both symbolic and representative of different sounds. In one translation the first quantity or letter is said to depict the head of an ox and is called "feoh" after that animal, the second is called "ur" after the word for bull, the third "thoru", a tree, followed by "os", a door; "rad", a saddle; "caen", a torch; and so forth. This was probably due to some fancied resemblance to the objects or, more likely, because the whole system was derived from a purely pictorial alphabet in which the pictures of the letters stood for animals or objects.

Another view is that because the runes were cut and not written there was some connection between the Anglo-Saxon word *secgan*, to say, and the Latin *secare*, to cut, especially where secret signatures are to be found, which were made by cutting a chip from the bark manuscript. For this reason also they contained no curves or elipses. In spelling, for example, the old sense of "spell" was a thin chip or shaving. Tacitus (A.D.98) goes into some detail about this as follows:

"To divination and lots they pay attention above any other people. Their method of casting lots is a simple one; they cut a bough from a fruit bearing tree and divide it into small pieces; these they mark with certain distinguishing signs and scatter at random and without order over a white cloth. Then, after invoking the gods and with eyes lifted up to heaven, the priest of the community, if the lots are consulted publicly, or, if privately, the father of the family, takes up three pieces one at a time and interprets them

according to the signs previously marked on them."

Bede refers to the casting of lots in the *Ecclesiastical History* as customary among the Saxons, as does the author of the old English poem *Andreas* with his specific mention of heathen practices:

"Casting lots they let them decree
Which should die first as food for the others.
With hellish acts and heathen rites
They cast the lots and counted them out."

This practice was referred to by later writers as the "Virgilian lots" and, although it sounds rather grim by modern thinking, doubtless the runes employed were supposed to indicate the karma of the one who was to die.

Runes and Sagas

The old Norse sagas are full of runic implications and contain constant references to the importance placed upon runic divination by all people from the ruler to the humblest peasant. Each runic sign was also said to stand for a nature spirit, and it was generally believed that to know which rune stood for which spirit or natural force gave the operator the right to call forth and seek the aid of the spirit in question. The late Prof. J. R. R. Tolkein incorporated the runic idea into his "Ring" saga and the rhyme goes:

"A king he was on a carven throne
In many-pillared halls of stone
With golden roof and silver floor
And runes of power upon the door."
                              (The Lord of the Rings)

In the Saga of Egill-Grimsson the runic episodes are fraught with magic. While at Thorfinnr's house Egill sees a sick woman and discovers that someone had placed a whalebone with the wrong runes in her bed.

"Then quoth Egil:
Runes shall a man not score
Save he can well to read them
That many a man betideth,
On a mirk stave to stumble.
Saw I on a scrapéd whalebone
Ten dark staves scoréd:
That hath to the leek-linden
Over-long sickness broughten."

Apparently the runes were then scored correctly and laid under the bolster in the resting place of the lady in question; she awakened from her sleep and declared that she was healed.

Above: *The tryfoss was a powerful symbol of the life-force in runic law. Its meaning is 'the will to create', and as in other great religions, the triad has divine significance.*

Other Symbols

Many other symbols have been associated with runic lore such as the tryfoss (the symbol of the Isle of Man) and the swastika. The former can be dated back some 700 years when it first appeared on the Manx sword of state which was said to have belonged to one Olaf Godredson, a Viking who used the sword when fighting the Moors in Spain. The swastika appearing amongst runes gives us some indication that there must have been a point in the distant past when East met West in magical culture. The Manx islanders also have a custom of making the tryfoss up in woven rushes and this they call the Cross of St. Bride (the Celtic goddess Bridget whose equivalent in the Greek pantheon was Athene and in the Egyptian pantheon, Hathor). An old German book tells us that the meaning of the tryfoss is "the will to create" and that it relates to the creation of the world. It is undoubtedly a life-force symbol in the same way as is the Egyptian ankh.

The Number Three

It is interesting to note how significant the "three' was in all ancient beliefs. The Druids acknowledged the sacred triad in their symbology and the Egyptians always presented their gods in trinities. From this we are, I assume, to draw the significance of two forces uniting to produce a third. The old Teutonic runes were 24 in number but later the Anglo-Saxons and some Scandinavians added another 9. These were purely for purposes of communication, however, and contained no magical connotations. The 24 runes which were magical were divided into three lots of eight, each lot of which was assigned to a god. These were called Freya's Eight; Hagal's Eight; and Tiw's Eight. But runes were sacred to one god in particular and that was Odin.

Odin was called "Lord of the Runes" and was patron of all wisdom especially magic. The Anglo-Saxons knew him as Woden and that word is said to have been derived from the old Norse "od", meaning "spirit". According to Tacitus, Odin was one and the same deity as Mercury, Hermes or Thoth, which speaks for the constancy of the archetypes throughout all the pantheons. Odin, although considered by the Norsemen as father of all, was himself subject to the power of fate, which force was personified

THE RUNES

Freya's Eight	ᚠ ᚢ ᚦ ᚨ ᚱ ᚲ ᚷ ᚹ
Hagal's Eight	ᚺ ᚾ ᛁ ᛃ ᛇ ᛈ ᛉ ᛊ
Tiw's Eight	ᛏ ᛒ ᛖ ᛗ ᛚ ᛜ ᛟ ᛞ

Above: *The original Teutonic set of runes were 24 in number. They were divided into three groups of eight, dedicated to the well-known Scandinavian gods, Freya, Hagal and Tiw.*

by a mysterious goddess or sometimes three goddesses in one. This Great Mother was senior to all the gods and her Nordic name was Wyrd, which the Scots later adapted as "weird", meaning "fate". Apparently, Odin had only one eye which was blue in colour, having bartered the other for the gift of wisdom. He wore a long blue cloak, carried a spear and rode a magical horse with eight legs called Sleipnir. He also had two pet ravens which always sat on his shoulder. Wednesday was the day of the week named after him, and of course all the days of the week are named after Norse gods. Tuesday was Tiw's day; Thursday, Thor's day; Friday, Freya's day; Saturday, the day of Saetur, Lord of the earth and fertility; Monday, Moon's day; while Sunday was sacred to Baldur, the beautiful Norse god of the sun who equates with the Greek Apollo. Since we use these names without thinking, it is good for us to be aware of the fact that the most common elements in life have magical origins.

Odin's Suffering

In the Eddic *Havamal*, Woden, the "High One", describes the passion and self-sacrifice which led him to the knowledge and wisdom of the runes. For nine nights Woden or Odin hung upon the world-ash Yggdrasil, wounded by his own

Right: *Odin, 'Lord of the Runes' and patron of all wisdom, especially magic. He shares this patronage with Mercury/Hermes, his equivalent in the more familiar classical panteans. He was always accompanied by his two pet ravens.*

scratched on all and sundry in those past days.

In the old Norse religion the idea of reincarnation and karma was accepted as it usually is in most beliefs which have a magical background. It is interesting to note that Iceland has recently reinstated the old Norse religion as the State religion; believers in the Norse Gods were prohibited from practising their faith when Christianity took a hold in that country around A.D. 1000. One of the beliefs of this religion is in the Yggdrasil, or Tree of Life, a fabulous tree which is said to stretch from the highest heavens to the lowest depths of hell. The sun, moon and stars hang upon its branches and it is cared for by the Norns or goddesses of fate. The tree theme also appears in the Qabalah, where it assumes a more abstract form, but the principle is the same. There is undoubtedly a similarity between the runes, the *I Ching* or ancient Chinese form of divination and the Egyptian Tarot which again could indicate some common

Below: *A medieval viking stone of the Gotland type represents a scene from Valhalla, home of the Norse gods. It contains magical symbols of the Norse religion.*

Above: *The huge, red-bearded figure of the god Thor, hero of warriors strides through the sky, brandishing his magical hammer, defending gods and men from the threat of giants.*

weapon, tormented by pain, hunger and thirst, until at last he spied the runes and with tremendous effort grasped them before he fell. And so he grew to strength and wisdom. There is also reference in the sagas to victory runes, thought runes, fertility and love runes, battle runes and so forth, so it would appear that Odin and his followers could employ them for divers purposes. One ancient script credits runes with the power of resurrecting the dead. Imbued with such powers, it is little wonder that runes were

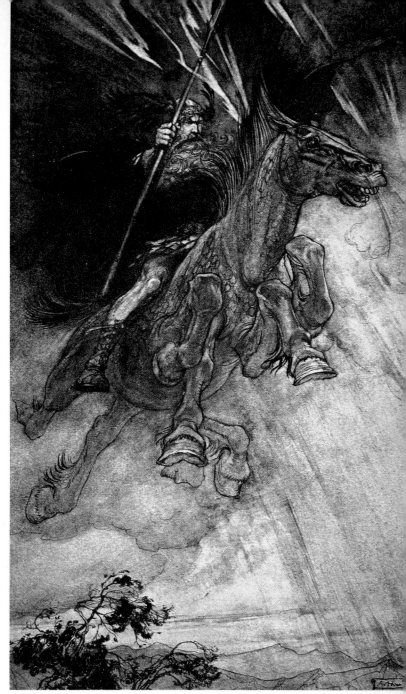

Right: *British artist Arthur Rackham depicted Woden raging across the sky.* **Top:** *This bronze viking helmet is engraved with protective symbols to guard the warrior.* **Below:** *An amulet, shaped like Thor's hammer was thought to provide divine protection.*

origin. Runes were in use in neolithic times, apparently, and runic lettering dating back to this period has been found in Alvao in Portugal.

The Language of Magic

Runic writing must have originally been a special language for the magically endowed, for as a system of writing it was quite unsuitable for lengthy or running communications. After the advent of Christianity it was quickly replaced by an Irish form of the Latin alphabet. The early fathers saw in the runes a link with the magical religion of the pagan past and hastened to stamp out their use as they also did the Celtic Ogham, which was another form of communication often used for magical purposes. Ogham was named after Ogmius, the Celtic god of learning and eloquence, and its alphabet, if one could call it such, was made up of a series of strokes. Similar again was the Bobileth or tree writing where every letter was named after a tree and the characters themselves were described as "twigs". The famous Welsh Bard Taliesin was obviously referring to this when he said, "I know every reed or twig in the cavern of the Chief Diviner." These twigs were often mistaken for runes and, although there are basic similarities, the two systems are quite distinct.

Long after the advent of Christianity Norsemen engraved runes on their swords and cups, believing firmly that these would protect them in battle and ward off evil and for years runic and Christian symbology went side by side in Scandinavia and the Anglo-Saxon countries. Just as today we have the rhyme "Thirty days hath September" etc., for helping us to remember the number of days in each month, the old Norsemen had a similar poem which helped them to recall runic meanings. The only known manuscript of this was destroyed by fire in 1731 but fortunately someone had the good sense to make a copy which was published by George Hicks in 1705. This has been reproduced many times since and can be found in a work entitled *A Sourcebook of the History of the English* by A. E. Farnham. In this work each runic character is the first word of a verse of the poem.

Casting the Runes

Casting the runes meant a method of throwing them down in order to calculate the future. They were "thrown at" the person when a magical spell was worked through them. Another interpretation of casting was that the same characters were used for both numbers and letters as the V, X and C are used in Latin. The "slivvers" of wood upon which the runic symbols were inscribed were often referred to as "bones". Runes were the symbols which connected man with spirit; they acted as a magical bridge as it were between the conscious and sub-conscious minds. This bridge could equally be utilised by a communicating entity or spirit who wished to give a message, or by the magician when astrally projecting through the time/space barrier. In pre-Nazi Germany there was a revival of interest in rune-magic and an attempt was made to link rune symbols with the heraldic symbols of Europe. We could dismiss this with prejudice but, on the other hand, there is some grain of truth in

Below: *A Norse long ship preserved in the University Museum, Oslo. The characteristic runic design is clearly visible in the carving on the prow.*

it as each rune has its own vibration and each person, country or part of the planet also has a "name by vibration" which is the sound, as it were, of their spirit. There were what could be described as runic mantras, or groups of runes which together made up a certain sound of a magical nature, rather like the mantras of the Eastern schools of occultism which are so popular today.

Runes in Magic

Runes were used ritualistically in the magic of the past and there are certain Orders today who employ them for this purpose. By the use of a runic inscription the Magus can work the power of his will either for good or evil according to his intention for, like all magical forces, the runes are totally impersonal, their power being coloured only by the intentions of the operator using them. When a runic inscription is drawn up by magical means it is written on a piece of paper or similar and must be handed, by the Magus, to the person for whom the spell is intended. It must also be accepted by that person into their hands; in other words, you can't slip one into someone's pocket. If not thus handed and accepted the runic working will be ineffectual. If a rune-cast is found, say, on a pavement by someone else it will not harm or affect him in any way for it can only become active when accepted by the person for whom it is intended.

The question which is bound to arise is: how can one escape from a rune-cast once accepted? A person who is handed a "yfelrun", which literally translated means a bad rune, can avoid the consummation either by meeting the requirements of that rune, for there are usually some conditions attached such as that if you do not comply with such and such a request then X will happen to you, or by handing the rune-cast back to the person who gave it to him in the first place. It may only be handed to the originator and not to a third party, but one can use subterfuge. For example, the rune-cast may be placed inside a book and the book given to the person, or the book may be placed in a position where the person will be the next one to pick it up and does so within sight of his erstwhile victim and within an hour of the book having been planted. This "throwing back" the runes will not work under any other conditions and, if you happen to be the unfortunate victim of an yfelrun and cannot return it, then you will need the help of a

High Magus to aid you avoid the consequences! Of course only magicians from the Left Hand Path throw bad runes, although it has been known for High Priests of certain Orders to give them to their pupils as a form of chastisement or from which to learn.

A Last Message

A strange story surrounds the assassination of the Russian royal family at Ekaterinburg. Hurriedly scratched on the wall of the room in which they spent their last moments were a set of runic looking characters which I am reproducing below in exactly the same way as they were seen by a British diplomat before the Soviets erased them. Rumour has it that the mysterious Rasputin dealt in both Tibetan and runic magic and that the swastika was the connecting link between the two. The message which the Czarina was trying to get over in such a hurry is anybody's guess, but there is little doubt that it had occult implications as the reader will observe.

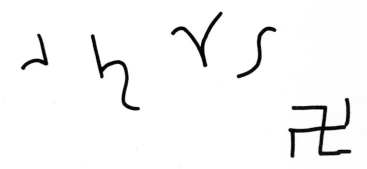

The Power of the Runes

These ancient runic symbols stimulate impulses from deep down in the collective unconscious mind of folk-memory and their effect, even upon disbelievers, is quite incredible. So the magician can use them for two main purposes, either to make a spell or to obtain some form of message. I would certainly advise that the former idea be dismissed unless the would-be thrower has a good knowledge of magic, for the rune-cast which does not reach its victim inevitably returns to its originator; this happens, of course, if the recipient of a bad-rune manages to slip it back to the person who gave it to him. For divination the runes are very good and I have devised a method of casting them which is based on traditional procedure and interpretations, but which can be used safely by any sensible and reasonably well-integrated person.

Above: *The famous 'Standing stones' of Callernish, are potent reminders of the Viking invasions of England.*

My own set of runes consists of 25 slivvers or pieces of wood, each one of which is inscribed with a runic letter with the exception of one which is left blank. Some modern mystics employ the 9 Anglo-Saxon runes in addition to the 24 Old German letters, but I find the originals far more potent magically so I stay with them. I have prepared two lists for the student. The first of these gives the accepted translations of runic glyphs together with the Old German and English names while the second picks out the 24 magical letters and assigns a divinatory significance to each one which can be used for fortune telling. From a comparison of these two lists you will be able to see how little the interpretations have changed in their deeper meaning so, while Nils Olaffson may have been worried about his horse casting a shoe in A.D. 700, our modern querent might be equally concerned about his motor car breaking down. The runic

meaning would be the same and only the terms of reference need to be re-shaped.

How to Use the Runes

Place a white or light coloured cloth in front of the querent and put the runic slivvers with the inscriptions facing downwards on a small piece of flat board or cardboard. Incline the board towards the querent's white cloth so that the slivvers fall upon it face downwards. Should any pieces turn during the operation they must be turned back again so that they are not recognised by the querent. The querent must then place the runes in a circle like the figures on the face of a clock with two slivvers at each point and the 25th rune in the centre thus:

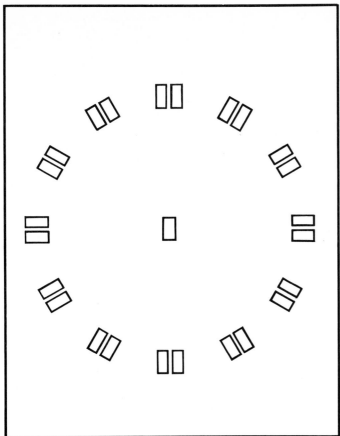

During this operation the runes must be kept face downwards. Starting at 1 o'clock turn the slivvers face upwards two at a time and read them in pairs; each one will relate to the next one to it. There is a definite right and wrong way up for some of the runes and if you are unfamiliar with the letters it is advisable to ensure that your set of runes is marked in some way so as to indicate the correct way up. Certain of the runes are the same both ways but in cases where a rune can be reversed there is a second meaning when it appears in that position. The blank rune stands for karma or fate and indicates that whatever is signified by its fellow rune cannot be escaped from or avoided. If the blank rune follows the double-triangle rune then death is indicated. The 25th rune, which is placed in the centre, stands for the querent and must be read as representing the trend which will affect him most during the period which is being enquired about.

Above right: *An example of 12th century runic writing left by the Vikings at Maes Howe, Orkney Islands, in the north of Britain.* **Below:** *An 11th century runic stone from Uppsala in Sweden.*

It is said that one can avoid the interference of malefic spirits during rune-casting if an invocation is made to Odin (Hermes or Thoth if you prefer to work in the Greek or Egyptian pantheons) and that this will ensure a lucid reading, a good understanding of the interpretation and safety from ill-wishers. As with all magical workings it is advisable to offer some form of prayer for protection and, from my own experience, I find it best to work within the pantheon involved which in this case would be the Nordic and the prayer would be to Odin or to the Great Mother.

Many methods of fortune-telling have almost been abandoned, because either they are no longer so familiar, or else fashion takes over, and one method becomes popular to the exclusion of others. The Runes are a very powerful method divination, and are not really 'difficult' as some people think. I hope that they will be used more.

Below: *The runes could predict specific events, such as natural hazards like this exploding volcano. Norsemen were well aware of the potent forces of nature.*

A Method of Interpretation

Glyph	Meaning	When in Reverse
ᚠ	Love fulfilled. Nourishment	Love frustrated
∩	An opportunity for advancement	A chance missed
♭	Do not make a decision, time will sort it out for you	A hasty decision which will be regretted
ᚨ	A gift from a parent or older person. A visit to or from same	An elderly person who will prove a nuisance
R	A journey undertaken for pleasure	Travelling which will interfere with plans
<	A lucky symbol for a woman, she will receive from the opposite sex. For a man, joy in giving	Loss or misplacement of something valued or a friendship
×	Uniting, union, partnership of some beneficial form	

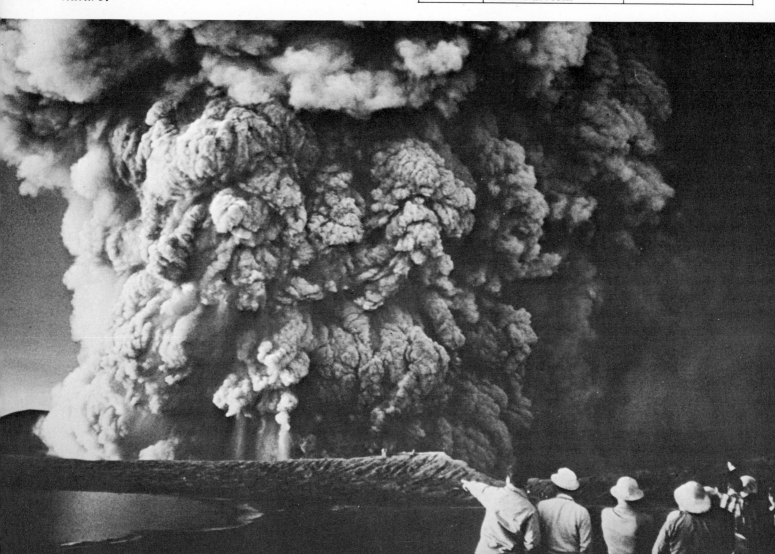

Rune	Meaning	Warning
ᚹ	Joy, happiness. Or a tall fair man who has recently travelled	Be careful in business matters for three days
ᚾ	Natural happenings could disrupt plans for the coming year. A message concerning same	
ᛏ	The need for constraint Go carefully in your plans	
ᛁ	A cooling off or an impediment of some sort	
ᛇ	One year ahead. A harvest or reaping of dues. A lawyer or professional man	
ᛆ	An inconvenience that will work out for the best. A difficulty averted	
ᛐ	Unexpected gains in material possessions	You expected too much and will be disappointed
ᛦ	A new and stimulating interest which causes you to use your mind	Don't get involved with people who will use you
ᛌ	You need to rest; be sensible and you'll soon feel fine	
↑	A man in love; if you are a male it will be you, if a female someone strong will love you	If a female, don't trust him; if a male, you won't stay with her long!
ᛒ	The family, a relative, a child	Worrying news concerning same
ᛗ	A change of dwelling for the better	A journey by sea
ᛜ	Don't sign a contract of any sort until after the next full moon	You have an enemy, the next rune will tell you how to handle them
ᚱ	The psychic rune. Intuition. Or an academic pursuit which will meet with success	Keep within your limits!
◊ or □	Completion of a project or a state of mind resolved	
⧓	An inherited possession, a will	Watch mechanical devices, they could cause a slight accident or some damage
⋈	A complete transition, or change of attitude of mind which results in a change of life style. Prosperity. If followed by the blank rune the change is death	
BLANK PIECE	The Path of Karma. That which is pre-destined and cannot be avoided. Matters hidden by the Gods	

Table of known translations of Runic Glyphs

Rune	Old German	Old English	Meaning
ᚠ	fehu	feoh	Cattle
ᚢ	uruz	ur	A wild ox. Strength, manhood
ᚦ	purisaz	porn	Thorn, Giant. Great spirit
ᚨ	ansuz	os	God
ᚱ	raido	rad	Riding. A journey
ᚲ	kaunaz kenaz kaino	cen	Torch fire. A protection
ᚷ	gebo	gyfu	A gift
ᚹ	wunjo	wyn	Joy, happiness
ᚾ	hagalaz	haegl	Natural forces which damage
ᛏ	naupiz	nyd	Necessity, constraint
ᛁ	isa	is	Ice. That which cools or impedes

Above: *Odin was a key figure in the Norse pantheon, and has inspired many artists to depict his exploits. Here he is shown at the tempestuous waterfall, by the artist and poet, William Blake.*

ᛃ	jera	ger	One year. Harvest
ᛇ	eihwaz	eoh	The hunting God Ullr. Avertive powers
ᛈ	perp	peoro	A secret or hidden thing
ᛉ	algiz	eolh (secg)	An elk. A sedge or rush. Defence, protection
ᛊ	sowulo	sigel	The sun. Life force
ᛏ	teiwaz	tir	The God Tir or Tiw
ᛒ	berkana	beorc	Birch twig. Fertility growth
ᛖ	ehwaz	e(o)h	A horse. Transport, moving
ᛗ	mannaz	man	A man
ᛚ	laguz	lagu	Water; fluidity, conduction
◊ or □	inguz	Ing	Ing, the God of fertility
ᛟ	opila	epel	Inherited possession or property
ᛞ	dagaz	daeg	Light, fruitfulnesss, prosperity

LATER ADDITIONS: ANGLO SAXON ONLY

	ᚪ	ac	ᚫ	aesc
	ᚣ	yr	ᛠ	ear
	ᛡ	ior	ᛣ	calc
	ᚸ	gar	ᛢ	cweoro
	ᛥ	stan		

THE CRYSTAL

Since the dawn of time man has been obsessed by an insatiable curiosity to know the future and this curiosity has led him to experiment with various forms of divination. Our modern dictionary defines the latter word as meaning "The art and practice of foreseeing and foretelling future events or discovering hidden knowledge". Even in this day and age this curiosity persists and modern man is just as anxious as were his ancestors to satisfy it, unless deterred by some form of fear. One of the most popularly employed methods of ascertaining the future is undoubtedly Crystallomancy, or crystal gazing as it is often called. The correct term for crystal gazing is scrying, a word which is derived from the Anglo-Saxon "descry" which means to see. Of course scrying as an art was in existence long before the Anglo-Saxons named it thus; in fact it has been part and parcel of man's experience on this planet since the dawn of time.

World Scrying

Scrying, in all its various forms has flourished everywhere in the world. Amongst the Greeks and Romans, the Hebrews, the Egyptians, the Babylonians and Assyrians; in India and China, Japan, Malaya and New Guinea, this method of divination has a long and colourful history. The Australian aborigines had, and still have, a healthy respect for a piece of crystal quartz, believing it to possess magical properties through which man can project his mind beyond the confines of time and space, and in New South Wales the natives actually worshipped crystals amongst other precious and semi-precious stones. This would seem to indicate the remnants of a much older and more advanced civilisation which had declined over the years, leaving only the skeletal remains of its true culture which was faithfully observed by those who followed on who were totally unaware of its former significance.

The Mayas certainly used the crystal and it was sacred to their god Tezcatlipoca. In Mexico there was a temple dedicated to this god the walls of which were entirely lined with mirrors. Mirrors made of obsidian or pyrites, generally the former, were habitually used for divination and for pronouncing judgment on criminals! The Incas also used mirrors for divination and the crystal was very popular with the Indians of North and Central America who used to polish up a specimen and consult it when they were worried about the future. The Apache Indians apparently used pieces of crystal to discover lost property and in particular lost or stolen ponies! Africa did its fair share of scrying in the past and, I am told, still does today. The Zulus had a special "Chief's Vessel" which, when filled with water, would divulge many hidden secrets both of the past and future, and the Matabales sought the answers to their problems by looking into pools of clear water.

Some Famous Scryers

In the 13th century Roger Bacon, that pioneer of scientific method, was obliged to submit to constant persecution, in spite of his scientific genius, on account of his occult and magical activities not the least of which was his interest in and use of the crystal for scrying. In most of the stories told of Bacon mention is made of a brazen head and magical glass which could speak to each other and see all things.

Dr. John Dee

Cornelius Agrippa was also renowned for his working with the crystal as was Nostradamus, that prince amongst seers, but the greatest of them all was undoubtedly Dr. John Dee (1527-1608), consultant Astrologer to Elizabeth I of England. Dee was a brilliant man even by today's standards. Amongst his attainments could be counted mathematics, astronomy, geography, navigation, calendar reform, secret service activities (he was the original 007) and, of course, the crystal for scrying which was his special interest. On 21st November 1582 he bought a crystal "as big as an egg; most bryght, clere, and glorious"; it was this fabled stone which served as the line of communication for his "angels" who taught him and watched over him and his Queen and country. Dee himself referred to this stone as the "shew-stone", although from his writings which have come down to us it was evident that he possessed many other crystals. Perhaps this was providential for, on one occasion when he was accused of

Right: *Medium Jeanne Dixon gazing into her crystal ball. She says 'I like to dream into it with lighted candles casting shadows behind me'. Jeanne forecasted the assassination of President Kennedy.*

magical practices and his house at Mortlake was invaded by the mob, several crystals were destroyed to the satisfaction of the angry witch-hunters. But apparently Dee always carried his favourite angelical stone on his person, no matter where his travels took him, so he could be assured as to its safety. This occasion was no exception and so the fabled crystal survived the angry mob unscathed.

The Devil's Looking Glass

Dr. Dee's crystal was not, however, the traditional clear stone but a black Mexican obsidian. After Dee's death the stone was said to have changed hands several times and in modern times one interested party traced it through a series of auctions to the collection of a famous literary lady in this day and age. From the description she gave to the gentleman investi-gator it would seem to be the original, about "as big as an egg". Horace Walpole, through whose hands it passed at one time, referred to it as "The Devil's Looking Glass" and hastened to dispose of it, but there is no record of it ever having brought ill fate to those who have owned it over the years since Dee's death. With the aid of this famous crystal and a scryer specially employed for the task, Dr. Dee compiled several volumes of information about all sorts of subjects. His best known contactee was supposedly the archangel Uriel, or Hermes Trismegistus, which genius was said to have supplied him with the necessary information which enabled the British to anticipate the arrival of the Spanish Armada. Queen Elizabeth would make no decision without first consulting her Court Magician, so the power and growth of the British Empire under that monarch must have

Below: *A beautiful piece of clear quartz in Dolamite, found in its natural state. Cut and shaped, it is a splendid medium for successful scrying.*

Right: *A colourful selection of finely cut and polished gem stones, including beryl, sapphire, tourmaline, garnet, zircon, peridot and many others.*

Above: *Dr Dee's 'shew-stone' in its case of stamped leather. Dee could not himself see the spirits called up with the aid of this 'Devil's Looking Glass', but had to employ a medium as scryer.*

owed much to Dr. Dee and his crystal. Other crystal gazers included William Lilly, who used to scry in a beryl set in silver; also, later, the notorious Cagliostro. Cagliostro was one of the characters involved in the happenings which preceded the French Revolution. He instituted a form of Hermetic Masonry which became popular amongst certain classes in France during the 18th century. In all his workings with a crystal he used a young boy as an intermediary.

The Three Categories
Crystals and mirrors of the divining sort can be divided into three categories:
1. The crystal or mirror which simply acts in an hypnotic manner as a focussing point for the clairvoyant or ESP faculty.
2. Those objects which are charged in some way so as to produce phenomena of the type which can reflect back a person's own subconscious state, or deflect energies of some sort or another on to the operator or querent.
3. Articles which are ensouled by some intelligence which does the work for the owner.
The first category is fairly straightforward to understand but the second category takes us into the realms of magic. A classic example of this is the sacred Egyptian Mirror of Hathor. The Goddess Hathor, legend tells us, was once entrusted with the sacred Eye of Ra through which she could see all things and, like the Greek Athene, she carried a shield which could reflect back all things in their true light. I happen to possess a Mirror of Hathor so I am fully aware of its potency. One side of it is used for scrying pure and simple and the other for viewing the inner soul. As with the picture of Dorian Gray it can store the lines of the true personality, id or alter ego, and the ancients considered the person who could look into this side of Hathor's mirror to be very brave indeed.

Objects can be changed by a magician to give them the properties enumerated under 2 above, but it is well to bear in mind that magical powers and psychic powers are not necessarily synonymous, as we shall see, and to be good at one does not guarantee success with the other. As for category 3, this can occur either naturally or through the intervention of a magician. For example, it is possible to discover a stone or crystal which is naturally ensouled by an elemental from the kingdoms of the earth devas or gnomes. If you possess the qualities which the gnomes most admire which are steadfastness, reliability, stability and industriousness then you will live happily with your crystal and it will serve you well. But should you not come up to scratch where your little friend is concerned, then woe betide you. Large powerful stones like the Hope Diamond are ensouled thus and were originally the property of trained priests and priestesses. When they fell into the hands of the uninitiated there was resentment from the ensouling entity or intelligence, who found that it could not respect the new owner. In fact, what happens is that the force within the stone is more powerful than the spiritual force of the owner and this has an unbalancing effect on the latter.

How to Scry
Professional operators will have their own methods of working but for the aspiring crystal gazer with little or no experience there are a few do's and don'ts. Your crystal should be kept scrupulously clean and you should not allow strangers to handle it except when you are going to scry for them. They should then hold it in their hands for a few moments. When using the crystal for scrying, it should be held between the

Above: *Dr John Dee. Dee was an innovator in both geometry and architecture in England, but he has been mocked for his unsuccessful magical experiments. Now we are rediscovering his beliefs.*

Above: *John Dee again, this time employed in an astonishing feat of mediumship in which he is raising a dead spirit, while protected by a carefully constructed magic circle.*

fingers and the thumb but if it is flat at one end it is best placed on a table, preferably on a dark background. Some crystals come with a holder which solves the problem. One legend has it that to 'see' over a long distance, one should look into the crystal sideways, but from experience I am inclined to take this with a pinch of salt. It does not really matter what size your crystal is and a large crystal does not necessarily give the best results. A good gem-stone, or a mirror, or even a glass of clear water will prove just as effective if correctly used.

By now the reader will have gathered that the crystal works one of three ways: by mirroring the sub-conscious mind of the scryer; by producing a form of self-hypnosis which releases the barrier between the conscious and sub-conscious minds or by attracting some form of spirit intelligence which releases the required information through the agency of the crystal. In olden days, magicians went to great lengths to ensure that they were not misled through any of these agencies. The spirits manifesting through their stone had to be of the right order and not some evil or mischievous intelligence bent upon causing trouble, and the Magus presiding at a scrying session was careful to see that his medium did not project too much of his own wishful thinking into the reading. Rules of this sort apply just as much today, and living in the technological age does not exempt the crystal gazer from the dangers to be encountered on his or her journeys out of time and space. It is necessary, therefore, to take certain precautions against both undesirable external influences and self-deception for, as with any psychic practice, it is possible to end up on one grand ego-trip.

Crystal Rituals

In ancient times safety-first measures were achieved through the operation of a ritual, usually long and complicated, which involved the use of certain flowers, perfumes, incense, magical instruments and the likes. For those who like to work strictly by the old text-books of magic I shall outline a working of this nature and follow it with a simple, but equally effective method which is closer to our modern way of living. The first crystal ritual comes from an old French Qabalistic manuscript and runs thus: "Those who desire to establish communication with the good spirits of the crystal must lead a religious life and keep themselves unspotted from the world. The operator must make himself clean and pure, using frequent ablutions and prayers for at least three days before he attempts to practise and the moon must be increasing. If he choose, he may have one or two wise and discreet persons as companions and assistants, but he and they must equally conform to the methods and rules of the art. The operator must be firm, strong in faith, great in confidence, and he must be careful that no portion of the ceremony be omitted if he desire to achieve success,

Right: *Queen Elizabeth I, resplendent in her jewels, employed Dr Dee as court astrologer. She made few decisions without his consultation.*

for on the exactitude with which the entire ritual is performed depends the accomplishment of his design. The invocant may perform the practice at any time of the year, provided the two luminaries are in fortunate aspect, in conjunction with fortunate planets; when the sun is in his greatest northern declination is said to be the best time.

In order to prosecute his work, the operator must have a small room in a retired part of the house, such as an attic or a low kitchen. It must be clean and neat, but with no sumptuous ornaments to distract his attention. The floor must be well scoured and quite level, so as to receive the lines of the several circles and characters which are to be traced thereon. The room must be free from intruders, from the hurry of business, and it should be locked when not in use. Every preparation belonging to the art must be made during the moon's increase. The operator must be provided with a small table, covered with a white linen cloth, a chair should be placed in the room and the materials required for a fire which will be necessary to enkindle the perfume proper to that planet which may govern the hour of practice. A torch, two wax candles, placed in gilded or brass candlesticks, highly polished and engraven, must be likewise provided together with a pair of compasses, and several minor accessories such as twine, a knife, a pair of scissors, etc. The magic sword must be made of pure steel; it must be supplemented by a wand of hazel wood, of a year's growth and a yard in length, graven with appropriate sacred characters. Every instrument, small or large, must be entirely new, and must be consecrated previous to use.

The most important adjunct of the practice is the crystal, which must be about four inches in diameter, or at least the size of a large orange. It must be properly ground and polished so as to be free from specks or spits, it should be enclosed in a frame of ivory, ebony or boxwood, also highly polished. Sacred names must be written about it, in raised letters of gold; the pedestal to which the frame is fixed may be of any suitable wood, properly polished. The crystal, like the other instruments, must be consecrated before being used, and should be kept in a new box or drawer, under lock and key. The names to be engraved on the frame are, at the North, TETRAGRAMMATON; at the East, EMANUEL; at the South, AGLA; and at the West, ADONAY. The pedestal which supports the frame should bear the mystical name SADAY, while on the pedestals of the two candles, ELOHIM and ELOHE must be respectively embossed.

In consecrating all instruments and other accessories of the art, the invocant must repeat the forms of consecration while imposing his hands upon the different articles, and his face must be turned to the East. The consecration being ended, he may then arrange the table with the crystal thereon, together with a candlestick containing a wax candle at each side of the circle, which should be seven feet in diameter, and must enclose a mystic square, whose angles at the apex point must, in each case, impinge the circumference. Both figures must be appropriately inscribed with sacred names and mystical characters and symbols. When the operator enters the circle with his companions, if any, it must be the day and hour of Mercury, the moon increasing, and the operations must be prefaced by an earnest invocation of VASSAGO, who is the genius of the crystal.

If the conjuration be often repeated, if the operator be patient and constant in his perseverance, and not disheartened or dismayed by reason of any tedium or delay, the spirit it is affirmed by the ritual, will at last appear, when he must be bound with the Bond of Spirits, after which he may be conversed with freely. "That this is a true experiment, and that the spirit hath been obliged to the fellowship and service of a magic artist heretofore, is very certain", says the same authority, but as all aerial spirits are very powerful, it will be well for the operator not to quit the limits of the circle until a few minutes after the apparition has been formally licensed to depart."

A Modern Approach

So much for the way they did it in preceding centuries. Now let us see if we can translate this into terms which can be readily understood and carried out by the man in the street. As with all psychic work, it doesn't do to play around with crystal-gazing if you are under the influence of drugs or alcohol. Chemical imbalances in the human body attract unbalanced spirits, especially from the elementary spheres, and you might easily be taken for a psychic ride if you are unable to control what you invoke. So the first requisite is a clear mind combined, of course, with clean surroundings.

With all magical work a short meditation is advisable beforehand. It helps to clear the mind of extraneous worldly matters so that the psychic forces can manifest with clarity and accuracy, unhindered by personal resentments, animosities, or the frustrations of the day. A good symbol to meditate upon is the Chalice or Grail. It is archetypal and can be found in most religions. In Hermeticism it is sacred to the Goddess Nephthys, The Revealer; in Christianity it is evocative of the cup from which Christ drank at the Last Supper and in Celtic Mythology it represents the Cup of Wisdom.

When you have meditated for a few moments and are feeling quite relaxed, place a protection around yourself and those present. If you can all tune in together to do this so much the better. This protection may be achieved either by the power of thought, i.e. visualising a golden orb which completely encases you all and upon the top of which is a sacred symbol such as the cross or ankh, by saying aloud the prayers of your particular religion if you follow a specific faith, or by a spontaneous call to your own personal concept of God, asking for protection from all malign forces during your use of the crystal.

Further Precautions

Now here come some more safety-first measures. Having finished with the crystal, all present should sit back quietly and make a mental picture in which you are being slowly encased in a beautiful blue mist. Imagine the mist rising gently about you until it finally closes over your head. This will have the effect of closing your aura so that once your circle is broken you will be securely sealed against any entity who might have been lurking about with evil intent outside your circle of protection. It is also advisable to place a 'thought protection' of this nature around the crystal itself before you put it away in its container, and just to be on the safe side (especially if it happens to be the room that you sleep in) pass your protective veil across the whole room.

Mention was made earlier of dedicating instruments which were to be used for a working and, of course, dedicating the crystal itself. Those who are practitioners of magic will have their own

methods of doing this, and it is not for such people that I suggest the following: take your crystal in your hand and sit quietly down. Meditate for a moment or two to clear and calm your mind, and say a prayer according to your belief. Hold the crystal to your forehead and as you do so, ask for the protection of a specific deity or angel. If you have no special beliefs I would recommend you to the Goddess Nephthys; if you are a Christian, the Archangel Gabriel, and for the magically inclined there are plenty of appropriate intelligences to invoke. One very able crystal gazer I know has dedicated his orb to that prince of diviners, Apollo. What we are really trying to establish is that your stone is placed under a benign protection, so that undesirable influences may not penetrate it to cause trouble and mis-inform you when you scry.

Above: *Scrying in Africa.*

Other Scrying Methods

In addition to the crystal, the main methods of scrying are with the use of some form of precious or semi-precious stone, a magic mirror or simply by employing a glass or container of clear water. Let us take each of these in turn and consider a safe and satisfactory method for their

Left: *The lily is the flower sacred to Nepthys, and should be displayed in scrying rituals in which she is invoked.* **Below:** *Nepthys, the Egyption goddess known as 'the Revealer', she is also queen of the Ondines, the water spirits who are the communicating mediums in water scrying. Nepthys is a most powerful goddess for divination purposes, once she is successfully invoked.*

use. Firstly, a gem-stone. The best stone is, I am told, one of the beryl group. *Avoid man-made stones*, i.e. those synthetically produced. Any jeweller will be able to tell you whether your stone is natural or synthetic so it would be advisable to make this check before employing this method of divination. Stones are sacred to the elemental spirits of the earth which are known in occultism as 'Gnomes'. These intelligences, which are part of the forces of nature, are said to reside in certain stones. If you possess a fine jewel stone, it is likely that there is some natural intelligence associated with it, so should you wish to use it for divinatory purposes it is advisable to court the favour of the entity.

Method for Scrying in the Jewel-Stone
Prepare for your scrying session in the same way as given for the crystal. Firstly, a short meditation, secondly, put up your protection either ritualistically, by prayer or by the power of your mind and thirdly, ensure that your jewel-stone is placed in a convenient position within your circle of protection. Here is an old Prayer of Exorcism, taken from the works of the French Qabalists, which is said to effect the harmless co-operation of any devic or elemental spirit residing in a stone:

"I beseech thee, oh creature of the kingdoms of earth, in the name of the Most High God, that thou should'st render unto me such services as I

Below: *The Egyptian goddess Hathor, to whom mirrors were sacred, is particularly helpful in scrying with a mirror. She represents a double-sided force, showing the balance of good and evil to the scryer.* **Right:** *A modern mirror of Hathor, made by the magical craftsman George Alexander, is based on the original mirror of Hathor, which is displayed overleaf.*

shall request of thee, being within the bounds of Universal Law, and that thou should'st refrain from deception, nor step from thy rightful sphere to interfere in the ways of men; only that thou should'st aid in as far as thy powers permit. In return for this good office I offer thee a true acknowledgement of thy beingness, and the Love of the Almighty and His Angels. So mote it be.''

This sort of old prayer can of course be translated into modern terms and merely consists of a request in the Divine Name followed by a warning to the spirit in question that it would be inadvisable for it to step beyond the bounds of Cosmic Law or interfere with the decisions of men by giving false information. In olden times, some small gift was made to intelligences of this sort who gave assistance to men, but in modern magic an acknowledgment of their existence, together with a thought of love for them as being one of the branches of the Tree of Life is considered sufficient, and I have slightly adjusted the prayer at this point. In some magical systems, however, offerings are made to intelligences who assist with workings.

The jewel-stone is used for scrying in the same way that the crystal is employed. The facets may show more than one picture at a time, especially if your room is lit by candles which is the best method of illumination other than pure daylight. The colours for this ritual are greens and browns and the incense burned should be sandalwood. Ferns or leafy branches would provide adequate magical decoration. After working a ritual of this sort great care should be taken to dismiss any elemental spirits who have been called in to help, and the old French prayer of Dismissal and Thanks goes as follows:

"Because thou hast diligently answered my demands, and been ready to come at my first call I do here license thee to depart unto thy proper place, without injury or danger to man or beast; depart, I say, and be ever ready at my call, being duly exorcised and conjured by sacred rites and magic; I charge thee to withdraw with quiet and peace, and peace be continued betwixt thee and me, in the name of the Most High God . . ." (etc., according to your religion).

Giving Thanks

The thanksgiving factor in any psychic consultation is most important. If one has been helped by an external intelligence, it is not simply a piece of conventional behaviour to say 'thank you' for the implications of a just acknowledgment reach far beyond the bounds of the petty customs and fashions of men. Of course it is not necessary to repeat such a complicated and verbose prayer as is given above and you can always put the theme into your own words or thoughts. Man is inclined to do too much taking in this universe and very little giving in return, and it is as well to bear in mind that when he takes more than is his due, it will sooner or later rebound on him. After the intelligences have been thanked, the procedure for closing the aura should be carried out before the circle is broken, as with the crystal. Now let us consider scrying into a glass or container of clear water. The method is much the same as for the stone, except that it will be the elementals of Water, or Ondines, who will be invoked. Of all the spirits of the elements the Ondines are the most psychic. Nephthys is their Queen, although she has been given many names in mediaeval magic as have all the gods. Necksa is probably the one she is best known as in old magical scripts in her capacity as sovereign of the Kingdom of Ondines, the spirits of water.

Method for Scrying into Water

The old French prayer to the Ondines is similar to that used to exorcise and invoke the Gnomes

and runs thus: "I beseech thee, oh creature of the element of water, in the name of the Most High God, that thou should'st render unto me such services as I shall request of thee, being within the bounds of Universal Law, and that thou should'st refrain from deception, not step from thy rightful sphere to interfere in the ways of men; only that thou should'st aid in as far as thy powers permit. In return for this good office I offer thee a true acknowledgment of thy beingness, and the love of The Almighty and His Angels. So mote it be."

Again you may word this as you will as long as the theme is maintained and the necessary precautions adopted. The colours for the Ondines are pale blue and greeny blue, flowers should be the periwinkle or branches of vervain or ash, and saffron should be burned as an incense. The prayer of thanksgiving and dismissal is the same as used for the Gnomes if you want to keep to the old magical formulae, and the session should be completed with the sealing of the aura and general clearing of the room. Containers used for water in scrying should be kept scrupulously clean and the water which has been scryed into must be poured away *immediately* the working is finished. This is most important.

Finally, let us look at scrying into a mirror. One can, of course, purchase mirrors which have been made especially for this purpose, I myself have a Mirror of Hathor. But here we are entering the realms of serious magic once again and, as I have already emphasised, it is advisable to leave these alone unless you are prepared to study the subject seriously. For the beginner who wants to scry into a mirror here is a simple way of going about it.

Method for Scrying into a Mirror

Obtain a small mirror — a very large one is not a good idea for this work. It should have a small stand attached to it so that it can be faced in any direction required. Ensure that your mirror is only used for scrying and is not soiled by having hair combed over it or the likes. Keep it securely hidden away in a soft cloth when not in use. It should be consecrated to Hathor, the Egyptian Goddess to whom mirrors were sacred. Here is a short prayer of consecration which might help you if you have no ideas of your own as to how to approach this diety:

"Great Goddess of Wisdom, Nourishment and

Protection, who is called Hathor by the students of wisdom but who is lion-headed to the profane, we pray you to protect this mirror with which we seek to probe the regions of timelessness, and to stand guardian against the forces of deception who seek the destruction of men. May our minds be shown only those things which are rightful for our true karma and may we be granted the wisdom to interpret what we see with logic, balance of mind and true understanding. So mote it be."

I have simplified this from an old Egyptian invocation but let me issue a word of warning. Hathor represents a double-sided force, and while she may help the scryer to see pictures of the future, or to project to some distant place, she may also show him the truth about himself, which can be devastating if he is not an integrated personality! So it is advisable to understand that man does not have full command of these faculties of intuition and revelation, in fact he is only on the threshold of understanding how they function and the laws involved in their use. I cannot emphasise sufficiently the caution which should be exercised in this sort of work.

Your mirror should be placed on a table of medium height and a candlestick containing a pink or orange coloured candle should be placed each side of it. The reader should not try to scry by looking directly onto the mirror, but should sit slightly to the side and look *across* the mirror. If possible, your mirror should face a blank wall, and care should be taken that it does not reflect the images of those present in the room. A good idea is for those who are sitting in on the working to be seated each side of the mirror, so that only the reader has the mirror face in full view. The circle of protection should be drawn so that the mirror is the central point, but care should be taken that all present are closed within the circle. Hathor's colours are coral, apricot and pink and her flower, like the incense best suited to the occasion, is rose.

If the working is successful and pictures are seen in the mirror a prayer of thanks should be offered to Hathor. If you are at a loss for words, the following was after the fashion of the old Egyptian thanksgiving:
"We thank thee, Great Hathor, for the protection afforded and for the information granted. Help us to use it wisely for the good of all things within the Universe of the Most High." Auras

should then be closed and the clearing made as previously described. Having covered a few methods, the question is bound to arise as to what can be done if no results are obtained from any of them. This is, of course, highly possible, for unless one of those sitting in the group is psychic or receptive it is doubtful whether any impressions will be received. If a particular combination of persons does not produce results, I'm afraid you will just have to change around until you find someone who has the necessary receptivity to see the images in the crystal, stone, water or mirror you have chosen to employ for your scrying. It will not take much experimentation to find out who is or who is not psychic. I have found that there are more psychic-receptive people about than there are of the outgoing-directive types who are more suited to the work of the magician. If you find that this sort of activity upsets you in any way, either physically or psychologically *then you must stop*. The psychic does not suit everyone, and to carry on just to appease your ego can only bring you trouble in mind and body.

Above: *The Egyptian mirror of Hathor the original of the one made by George Alexander, is displayed in the British Museum.*

THE TAROT
FOR
❧ LIFE ❧

Left: *Samson is shown forcing open the jaws of a lion in this 16th century stained glass window. Conceivably, traditions overlap, for card 11 in the Tarot, called 'The Enchantress' depicts the same struggle of spiritual versus physical strength.*

Above: *The Tarot cards are not related to any particular country in terms of their origins, and their designs are likely to be modified by various national influences. However their basic symbols remain constant, as in this French pack.*

The Tarot, in so far as it is known to the public, is invariably associated with fortune-telling. The Bible is often opened at random for use as an oracle, but we would not think of it as a book expressly for telling fortunes; neither should the Tarot be so regarded. The twenty-two keys of the Tarot enshrine a miraculous doctrine in pictorial form, concerning the nature of the essences of life. Understanding these symbols provides us with a teaching of how to overcome decay and death; how to evolve to perfection in fact, so that our bodies would undergo a series of transformations that would change the molecular structure of cells, subjecting them no longer to the horrors of deterioration.

True universal laws of life naturally apply to the individual, the macrocosm and the microcosm, therefore a random choice of cards can tell us where an individual is in relation to the essences of life. The pattern made by the involuntary choice of cards must be interpreted by a skilled diviner however. Also, it is an absolute law that "we get what we are". This means we get the kind of life, luck and experience consistent with the types of consciousness we are cultivating and using in life. Our bodies have a consciousness of their own, so what we call random choice is very often the body asserting its wisdom. To give just a hint about body consciousness, when we have learned to swim, ride a bicycle, drive a car, or any similar set of particular body movements, we say we do it automatically. This is not really true. These complicated movements are taken over by a consciousness centred in the body, so that once the skill is learned, it requires no further instruction from the head. All too often there is a serious breakdown in communications between the body and the head. Witness the advanced state of many diseases in the body before the head knows anything about them. So when we shuffle cards or pull a few out of the pack at random, this is often a chance for knowledge contained in our bodies to communicate itself to our heads (provided we can interpret the symbols correctly). Sometimes when I am reading a fortune I have the sensation of crudely reading what is on the part of the 'tape' which has not yet been played. As if the seeds of the future of a person is already within them, and if they could get in touch with these seeds, they would not only know what was going to happen, but if they were strong, could alter the 'script'.

Most fortune-telling tacitly says is, "If you go on as you are, this and this is likely to happen to you". Never let it be forgotten that should a person find the means to significantly change his or her approach to life, a new pattern could open up for that individual. It is sad to report that very few of us indeed ever manage to break our habitual responses to life, and thereby lay down an all too depressingly predictable pattern for our future, which even includes its surprises.

Above: *The pack used throughout this article is known as the Horus or English pack. The card shown is called The Sun.*

Right: *Aleister Crowley, self-named 'The Great Beast' employed Frieda Harris to design a pack to his own specifications.* **Overleaf left:** *The Magician from the Crowley pack is shown here, and* **Overleaf right:** *a display of the Major Arcana from the pack.*

The conscious mind is a great trickster and manipulator. It tends to take possession of us and dominates us on its own terms, blinding us to many other aspects of our being. It is not surprising therefore that it is symbolised by the Juggler in the Tarot. "Men are deceivers ever" said Shakespeare. The conscious mind is essen-

tially masculine and the Juggler depicts its first essential principle, intelligent initiative. He stands there demonstrating his skill and maintains the illusion that he knows it all. No single symbol in the Tarot has such comprehensive knowledge. However it behoves us to appreciate the qualities he can bestow. It is intelligent initiative that has founded every industry and enterprise we have ever known. Too often, people without his gifts presume that they are entitled to rewards that are strictly his by right of the risks that he has had the courage to take. The man who lacks courage to risk independent action forfeits his right to great rewards.

The Juggler can also teach us about love. To really cope with and affect the female, a young man must be able to prove his skill and courage. This draws some degree of Solar consciousness into him. In fairy stories, which seem to know more about our essential nature than most other forms of literature, the young man is not allowed near the princess until he has proved himself. If he cannot do this he has no chance of transforming his love, nor she of transforming him. All he can do is to make her pregnant, without changing his own consciousness or that of the woman. Magical transformative love-making is taught in the first four symbols of the Major Arcana of the Tarot, so perhaps we should look at them in sequence. Card 2, the Priestess, symbolises the virgin. She is the Sleeping Beauty of the fairy story with her intuitive knowledge hidden behind the veil

stretched between the two pillars and rolled up in her secret book. She awaits a Prince Charming with the fire, intelligence and courage to awaken her potential power and wisdom. Poor girl she still waits. How many men today seek to enhance their effectiveness? The true female is a priestess of love with the intuition to guide her how to draw the very essence of the male into her, transform it and return it to him and thereby transform herself. Today she is a tragic figure without hope, as we seem no more to produce great men.

Card 3, the Empress is the goddess of all fruition and all creative arts. Some aspects of her powers can manifest in us as we manage to integrate some portion of our male and femaleness within ourselves, or this integration can be

Card 5, the Hierophant is the symbol of the spiritual guide which is lit by the spark of consciousness that bridges the gap between Heaven

brought about by a male being sufficiently masculine to transform the Priestess into the Empress, bringing her attributes to both of them. She bestows gifts which flow from integrity.

Card 4, the Emperor, symbol of temporal power and authority, a further gift which the Priestess can bestow upon the male worthy and able to penetrate to her essence. She brings true power and realism to the superficial youth who thought he knew it all. Such integration of male and femaleness can be also achieved by the technique of developing male and female functions in oneself and then uniting them by deep meditation. So the way of our further evolution is either to develop all our male and female functions (a long and difficult job) then join them within, or have females evolve the feminine functions and the males the masculine ones, so that when they come together in love, a perfect union is achieved which unites and transforms the essence of both.

and Earth. He is the great teacher, and as such let us allow him to do a little teaching. The reason why the fifth card is the number of great teaching is because it represents that which is born from the integration of the four elements of consciousness, and as such possesses a spark of super-consciousness. Most of us live in states of elementary consciousness, but if we could cultivate and integrate ourselves, then a spark of etheric or super-consciousness could begin to grow in us. Then we would become more aware of the will of God. Having this spark of etheric consciousness is the real distinction between a true clergy and the laity.

The Hierophant stands next to card 6, the Lovers and represents love, choice and tempta-

tion. No one can be a hierophant who does not know the nature of love, its needs and possibilities, as love is the only way to achieve our further evolution and become connected to Heaven once again. So love is the key to knowledge for the real hierophant. If he is not master of this mystery he is no hierophant and can do much damage by posing as one.

The Tarot cards are archetypal, that is they represent actual forces and entities in our

cosmos. They are not mere ideas. I must say this in an age where everything is regarded as a theory. The powers they represent are and were always around us, awaiting our evolution to find them and cultivate them in ourselves to an ever higher degree of perfection. When we first became aware of these powers we had vague ideas about them and made many mistakes as we tried to tune into them. We are still busy making these kind of mistakes. In the technical world for instance we have made the Juggler a god, calling him the scientist. Everything has to be scientific to be taken seriously. We don't seem to see that the Juggler contains no genuine wisdom, is not concerned with high human standards, does not foster the arts and possesses no super-consciousness, the first essential for human guidance. He has captivated us with his technological tricks and led us far astray from living according to our deeper human needs. This is what tends to happen when we find out how to tune into one of these archetypal powers. They so mesmerise us that we forget about the other powers and tend to reject anyone who does not tune into the same power as ourselves

Thanks to the physicists we now know that there is nothing concrete in the universe. All manifestation is energy clinging to itself in various patterns. This means that there is nothing which cannot be changed; all we need is a bunch of keys to transform matter to its highest forms. The keys of St. Peter take on a new meaning in this context. Card 7, the Chariot, represents above all else the impetus of our true progress. Our only true progress is towards becoming more highly evolved beings, hence we see him controlling two diametrically opposed forces. The two horses are completely opposite in nature, and on his shoulders are the faces of the conscious and subconscious minds whose needs and natures are in total opposition. Only from using and integrating these forces can he have any true control. Most of us are 'either or' kind of people so that we never get anywhere as regards evolving ourselves. To explain what this means in everyday life:- people say "I am like this and not like that." "I am logical and intellectual and have no time for that psychic rubbish". Or the other way around: "I am psychic and can't stand those intellectual idiots." Or "I'm practical and have no time for fun and carnivals." Examples are legion, but they all mean: "I am stuck in my rut and have no chance of evolutionary progress in this lifetime." He who denies the psychic world of intuition, telepathy, fortune-telling is denying the essential essence of femaleness. He who denies the intellectual world of science and logical deduction is

Card 11, the Enchantress often called La Force in French, is undoubtedly a most important symbol for us at this time. She represents

denying the essential essence of maleness. All denial is catastrophic to our well-being since all our attributes have a cosmic force behind them, and if we do not give them expression, sooner or later, they destroy the civilisation which does not allow them their path to earth through the people. True progress is always the cultivation of opposite qualities and their integration.

Card 8 symbolises justice and retribution. Above all else it symbolises balance, again the balance achieved by reconciling opposing forces. Like all the other cards of the Major Arcana it represents an actual cosmic entity which we have to develop to truly comprehend. Any study of history will show us the many and varied ideas we have had about what is just. Even today we could hardly claim to be giving this great Goddess true expression in our world. At present she seems to be seen more in terms of equality, than any true enquiry as to what may be just.

the ultimate in feminine power. As this form of power is so little known and even less respected in our time we very much need to be reminded of it. Her power is charm. All that can be achieved by irresistible charm is hers, and all men fear her, hence our determination to keep her suppressed. She can melt anything, even the proverbial stones. It is her power that produces apports (causing objects to move from one place to another without anyone touching them). The power to levitate is also hers because her power is based on metaphysical water, that blue vibration which surrounds our planet. She holds the secret of how to float up in it, so stories of magic carpets and flying broomsticks come from a time when we could tap her energies successfully. Uri Geller demonstrates what she represents, because it is an aspect of her powers with which he bends keys, affects clocks and so on. She softens the internal grip of molecules upon one another thereby rendering it simple to alter the shape of any object.

Note that both the Juggler and the Enchantress have the sign of infinity and immortality on their heads. In some packs the sign hovers just above the head, in others it is created by the broad brim of their hats. Indeed they are both key figures in terms of showing the possibilities of our gaining immortality. If we could develop both to a high degree in ourselves and unite them we would be well on our way. Conventional education caters almost exclusively for emphasising the Juggler in us. Officially, nothing whatsoever is done to enhance the power of the Enchantress in the individual. The values we need for enhancing her are in total opposition to the values we need to grow the Juggler.

Card 12, the Hanged Man; he hangs upside down to symbolise truth, for truth is so often the opposite of what everyone thinks it is. Invariably if someone sees the truth about something and it differs from popular opinion, he is told right away that he has got things the wrong way round. Seeing the truth on your own is a perilous state as this symbol suggests. You are likely to be opposed, isolated and made to feel uncomfortable in many ways. Truth is dynamic and very difficult for one person to carry on his own. If he cannot share his vision he may be broken by its force. Van Gough springs to mind in this context. No other artist that I am aware of saw and illustrated so well, the dynamic meta-

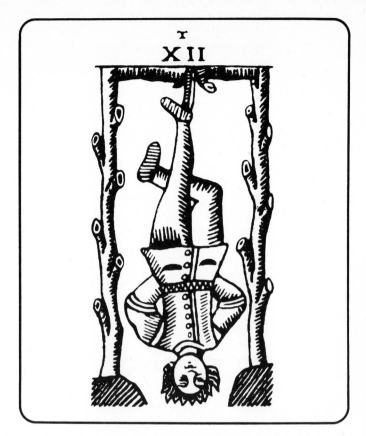

physical forces of life. How his trees hurtle out of the earth and the sun's power hurtles towards it. This vision was dynamic and real but none around him were sufficiently aware of these metaphysical forces. He could not share the truth he had seen, so the balance of his mind was often in danger. The Tarot is an instrument designed to teach us about the very forces that Van Gough depicted so well, the metaphysical vibrations of Earth, Air, Fire and Water, which give rise to all manifestation and surround us all the time. This is conveyed in Aleister Crowley's Tarot pack which vibrates with living energy.

Card 14, Temperance is the symbol for time and its activity. There she stands with her two vessels, one filled with sunshine, the other with rain. She pours them down upon us alternately that all may grow and prosper. The sun is the male force, the rain the female force. We rarely allow rain to penetrate into our metaphysical consciousness, and true femaleness in either sex is heavily discouraged, so our lives are dry and

Right: *Uri Geller, the young Israeli whose strange power over material objects is a demonstration of the power belonging to the Enchantress, the symbol of the 11th card of the Major Arcana.*

lacking in imagination. This is a very serious state of affairs, for great love cannot be achieved without a lively imagination. T. S. Eliot wrote *The Wasteland* to draw our attention to this dangerous state of affairs, but as in the case of most seers his message has been completely ignored, and we go blundering on from bad to worse in our blindness. Time must be allowed not only to perform her duties in the world, but in us too if we are to fulfil our destiny.

Card 21, the World represents life in a state of paradise. It is symbolised by a happy girl dancing in the centre of an intertwined oval garland which represents totally integrated elements. The symbols of the four elements appear at the four corners of the card. The Angel for water, the Eagle for air, the Bull for earth and the Lion for fire. If we could develop and integrate our four basic elements we would be back in a state of paradise. The Tarot is often regarded as the book of the Alchemists and card 21 represents the completion of the Great Work. The Great Work is to bring ourselves and thereby the world into a state of perfection. What a terrible price we have paid and are paying for the ousting of the alchemists by the materialistic chemists to whom they gave birth. All meaning

to life has been lost since the chemists took over. Alchemists were concerned with the metaphysical roots of things in the earth and in the cosmos, that is why they were so often great astrologers. The chemists concerned themselves with mere physical matter, and thereby lost the awareness of the true significance of everything. I am not referring to alchemists as the 'puffers' who spent their time trying to turn base metals into gold. Unfortunately chemists have conspired to make us believe that that was all the alchemists did. A close study of Paracelsus will help you to know something about alchemy.

We could say that the mother gives birth and meaning, and the father or the son gives knowledge and application. Unfortunately in three major areas the son has killed the mother. For instance numerology preceded mathematics to which it gave birth, but the son killed the mother so that numerology is no longer used in our lives. Thus the meaning of numbers has been forgotten, even though they represent cosmic

Right: *The poet T. S. Eliot, who, in his prophetic poem* The Wasteland *wrote of the essential ambivalence of all sexuality, and of the repression of the imaginative female qualities.*

forces and have a real significance whether we choose to ignore this or not. Astrology gave birth to astronomy, but again the son killed the mother and the influences of the stars and planets have been officially forgotten. Not many people realise that Newton who discovered the force of gravity was no mean astrologer. I have already described how the son chemistry has killed mother alchemy, and believe that the original truths should be revived in order that we may rediscover the sources of knowledge contained in them. It should be clear that knowledge comes to us first via receptivity and intuition, and this faculty should never be denied however mesmerised we may become by its latest birth.

In talking about the earth, her real needs and the kind of human life and behaviour she must sustain in order to bring her and us to a state of perfection, let us think of a few possibilities which could help her and ourselves. First, we must truly realise that our evolution is still in progress, therefore we should be open to major changes happening to us in our life-time. At present all establishments are psycho-static with laws based on the assumption that we are all always going to decay and die. Psycho-stasis is the universal disease which kills us and ruins our planet in so many ways. This is the first behaviour pattern we must change.

This gives rise to the need to devise more experimental ways of living. A practical start to this problem would be to divide countries into small, independent units. Each unit could have complete cultural autonomy to introduce any kind of life style it felt was worth trying. These realms could be loosely held together within a framework of economic co-operation, but culturally the more different they were from one another, the more successful the experiment would be likely to be. This would tend to counteract the present insignificance of the individual, which gives rise to so much negative behaviour.

Card O, the Fool is the symbol for God in the Tarot. O stands for nothing, No Thing, yet the circle also stands for everything, and is of great use to mathematicians to turn 1 into 10 or ten million. The true nature of the ultimate dynamic power is what we seek. Perhaps a starting idea to give us direction, is to look at, say a beautiful car. When we do this we tend to be mesmerised by its sleek splendour and the powerful engine.

However God is more akin to the fuel in the tank upon which all this marvellous achievement depends to give it any meaning, function or use. God certainly is volatile. Think of 'acts of God', they are very much akin to a petrol tank exploding! We have not yet learned to cope with this amount of dynamic energy in ourselves.

I do hope that this brief reference to some of the Tarot cards may give the reader some inkling of their extraordinary and miraculous power. The reason why they are not universally acclaimed is because we are not yet evolved enough to face the challenge of a life which is more abundant: let us hope that day may be soon in the coming. This civilization may now be in its death throes, so humanity may now begin to find the courage to live. So ignorant are we that history shows that we have only learned by disaster and then, not very much. It is time we ceased to regard the Tarot as some fashionable fortune-telling game and sought to learn the way to life through its dynamic doctrine. May I wish all readers every success in any quest they make towards more life. No matter who succeeds, from every true accomplishment we all are given a greater chance to evolve.

FRESH TEAS.

Divination has long been thought of as something mystical and even magical. The very word evokes thoughts of witches and wizards summoning demons and demanding knowledge of the future, but what about we other mortals who also want to know what fate has in store for us? There is little time for elaborate rituals and anyway, who wants to spend hours studying the stars or the entrails of animals, let alone have a conversation with a raging demon or one's aunt who has been dead for the last twenty years. The answer is simple — improvise; use those things with which you have the most contact. Those things which are part of your life as well as your future, which are easy to obtain and can be used without much fuss or bother.

It is not for nothing that England has been called a nation of tea-drinkers. To the majority, tea is a national institution, a necessity, a way of life. It may not be such an institution in other countries, but at least it is widely available in most parts of the world. Tea of course, is very old. It was used in China three thousand years before the birth of Christ, not only as a refreshing drink, but as a soothing, medicinal beverage. Tea arrived in England in the middle of the seventeenth century and was a luxury commodity. Until 1885, most of the tea was imported from China, but after that time India rapidly developed into a tea-producing country along with Ceylon and soon they became the biggest suppliers of tea to Britain and Europe. Even in Victorian times tea was treated with the greatest of respect and was often kept locked in little wooden boxes to stop the servants sampling the brew. Now the situation has very much changed.

Beverages for Divination

In view of its history, it is evident that tea-leaf reading, as such is a relatively modern form of divination. However, the Ancients divined the future by studying water and noting its colour, ebb, flow and the number of ripples produced by stones. This is called hydromancy and was the direct forerunner of our modern tea and coffee ground divination. The next step led to the study of wine dregs, which produced similar patterns to tea-leaves and was called olinomancy. Finally tea and coffee had arrived and their residue created a natural outlet for the divinatory faculty under the name of tasseography. The Victorian era saw many a group of anxious ladies huddled around the parlour table listening to their unfolding future and there were numerous tea-leaf readers before the 1940s. Since then, unfortunately, there have been fewer tasseographers around. Advertisements abound offering the services of palmists, Tarot readers, and astrologers, etc., but few tasseographers. Tea-leaf reading is a private matter shared among friends and relatives. Just as refreshment is not usually offered to complete strangers neither is this form of divination.

Spatial Clairvoyance

Tasseography has proved to be a very valid system of divination, so what exactly is it that makes it work? How and why do the leaves form themselves into the prescribed symbols? Why and how are we able to interpret them? The faculty used is E.S.P. — extra-sensory perception — knowledge gained by other means than through the normal five senses. In particular it is the sixth sense — clairvoyance that enables us to foretell the future in this way. There are several types of clairvoyance or clear-seeing, but the one used here is called spatial clairvoyance, which simply means seeing through both time and space as opposed to seeing ghosts or other spirits or receiving spiritual visions. The gift of clairvoyance is usually thought of as something you have been born with. In fact we are all born with this gift, but in the majority it is latent and needs to be developed. The more a person listens to the voice of intuition, the more "psychic" they become, and the same applies to divination. The more practice, the easier and more accurate it becomes as clairvoyance unfolds.

Why do the tea-leaves form themselves into picture-symbols? Is it pure coincidence or imagination? Nothing in this world is really a coincidence, despite what we might think to the contrary; the power or faculty that is used is called psychokinesis, which is a rather difficult term used to express the phrase "mind over matter" in a scientific way. Almost everyone knows that our minds are divided into two sections — the conscious mind and the unconscious mind. The conscious mind is the one that is usually functioning while we are awake. The events of the passing days are normally forgotten by the conscious mind, but they are all filtered through into the unconscious where they are stored for future use. The technique that brings this stored information back into the conscious mind ready for use is called memory, pure and simple. The two minds together act like a filing system or a computer. To complicate matters still further, the unconscious mind is further linked to what is called the collective unconscious. This may seem very confusing and you may think that all this semi-psychological anlaysis has nothing absolutely to do with fortune telling. However it is very important as it explains just how we are able to catch glimpses of the future. If you aren't interested in knowing "how" then you will never be able to tell your own future with any great accuracy.

The Collective Unconscious

The collective unconscious is like a long road which has the past at one end, the present in the middle and the future at the other end. Not only does this road contain things pertaining to you, but also to everyone else who has ever lived, is living at the moment, and who will be living in the future. The unconscious mind is your key to that highly educated road and it enables you to see the future by tuning into a particular section of the road at the directions of the conscious mind. You formulate your question in the conscious mind — "Does he love me?" "Is there any money coming to me?" "What does the future hold for me?" etc. This then filters through into the unconscious mind which then links into the appropriate portion of the collective unconscious, lifts out the information and then filters it back into the conscious mind. If this seems a little confusing, look at it this way; you feel cold so you want to put the electric fire on. Your conscious mind would be equivalent to you feeling cold and wanting to put the fire on; your unconscious mind would be the electric fire with its cable and connector. When the fire is plugged into the mains it makes contact with the electric power of the national grid — the collective unconscious. The feed-back starts the fire, which produces the heat and warms you up. Think about it, you'll soon get the idea.

Below: '*Cup-Tossing*' *by N. J. Crowley. The spilt salt indicates an unhappy fate is being predicted.*

Symbols: Personal and Impersonal

So, now you know the mechanism, what has it to do with tea leaves? To go back to psychokinesis, when the unconscious mind has the required information, it forms the tea-leaves into patterns and symbols for the conscious mind to interpret. Symbols can be rather confusing too. There are two kinds, personal and impersonal. The personal symbols are those having a particular meaning for a specific person. Everyone has their own symbols which have accumulated over the years by direct experience. For example, a man who had fallen from a ladder and broken his leg would always associate the symbol of a ladder with misfortune rather than with success; a person whose favourite hobby was archery would hardly associate an arrow with bad news; a person who has studied astrology or the Tarot would interpret the symbols by what they had learned and those of different social and religious backgrounds would have a variety of different interpretations for the same symbol.

Some people think of peacock's feathers as bad luck, probably by associating them as the "Evil Eye", while others think of them as symbols of protection as the peacock uses them to trick his enemies into thinking that there is more than one bird. To some, black cats are lucky, while others take them as a symbol of bad luck. Hence, there are many personal symbols with special meanings for different people. Impersonal symbols have no fixed meaning for you. A friend might associate an apple with stomach-ache but if for you, it has no particular significance, then it is an impersonal symbol for you. If you read your own leaves then you know what the symbols represent for you if they are personal ones, but you don't know your friends' personal symbols. This is where many of the problems lie in fortune telling. If you are a total beginner, it is best to name the symbol you see aloud so that your friend may comment on it if he or she wishes.

Intuitive Clairvoyance

The only real way to become a good tea-leaf reader is to develop intuitive clairvoyance, but of course, this takes time. However, the more you practice and the more you use your intuition in every-day life the better your results will be. When you read the cup, try to let your intuitive faculties function. It probably won't work at

first and you will have to be guided by personal symbolism and the impersonal symbolic meanings given later on. But do try to do without this list as much as possible. It is merely a guide and really to show the way to beginners only, and if you practice regularly you'll be an expert in no time. But you have to do all your own work, nothing comes easily and the sooner you can associate the symbols with everyday happenings automatically through your own intuition, the sooner you can call yourself a fortune-teller.

Curiously enough, the unconscious is very obliging. If you believe a symbol has a certain meaning, it will always turn up in that context. Your fortune is part of the present and the cup can warn you of danger, give you advice or tell you of happiness coming to you. Sometimes fate will give you a helping hand or a warning. What you do with the advice is your own affair. If you give someone a warning of unpleasant happenings in the future and they don't take your advice, don't be upset. It is their own fault if anything happens and they have the free will to do as they please. Always try to avoid telling someone extremely bad news such as a death. You could be wrong, and if you are right there may be nothing that could be done to avoid it. On the other hand people have been known to worry themselves to death. So do be a little bit tactful.

How to Read the Tea-Leaves

Now all the preliminaries have been taken care of, just how do you go about reading the tea-leaves? The first thing to get is a nice large cup with a plain white interior. If you use this cup only for fortune-telling then it will build up a strong association in your mind and as soon as you start to make the tea and use the cup your intuition will automatically begin to function. So, in a sense, the cup itself will actually become a personal symbol. Use tea with long stems rather than the fine powdery tea as you will get better symbols with the former. Obviously it's pointless to use tea-bags, although some people say that this is possible and that you can always break the bag open at the end. However the tea in tea bags tends to be rather fine and if you use proper tea in the beginning by the time you've finished drinking you should be in the right mood.

Even Distribution of Liquid

Make sure that you leave just enough liquid in

the bottom of the cup to distribute the tea-leaves around the cup; too much tea and the tea-leaves won't stick to the sides of the cup; too little tea and you won't be able to distribute the tea-leaves evenly. Once again, it's all a matter of practice. Having determined the correct amount of liquid to be left in the cup take the cup in the left hand and slowly twirl it three times. Then turn it upside down to drain in the saucer. If you are reading a friend's cup then he or she must do this on their own. During this time either a desire to know the immediate future or some specific question should be kept in mind. Before attempting to read the signs, the diviner should concentrate on the cup for a few minutes so as to get the imagination and intuition working to the full. The small ritual movements for distributing the leaves is basically to allow the unconscious mind to distribute the leaves in the cup into intelligible symbols by means of psychokinesis.

Seeing the Pictures

At first, the symbols may be difficult to distinguish, but by turning the cup in various ways and giving it the fullest concentration, the pictures should start to appear. If you get clear pictures straight away then you should have no difficulty in becoming a first class tea-leaf diviner providing you give your intuition time to work. Do not hurry, take your time. Accuracy is the most important. By tradition, you should read the cup from the left around to the right so as not to spoil the luck it may contain. A completely clear cup is said to be a sign of complete absence of trouble for the person concerned and is considered fortunate. However, it could merely be a sign that too much liquid was left in the cup! Starting from the handle, this represents the house and the home and the closer the symbols are to the right of the handle the sooner the events are likely to take place. Symbols appearing to the left of the handle represent the past or lost opportunities; the present and future is shown to the right of the handle. The bottom of the cup represents misfortune and bad luck. Leaves on the rim are significant of things happening in another location. All the following symbols must be modified according to their position in the cup in order to obtain correct results. Always start with the clear, easy discernable symbols first and then go on to the more difficult ones.

Below: *This Victorian group is reading coffee grounds. All forms of tasseography were in great vogue during the Victorian period.*

Geometrical Symbols

Geometrical symbols are the easiest to interpret and these have a tendency to appear more often in the cup.

CIRCLE: Indicates something completed and continuous happiness. If the circle is broken or there is a stalk crossing it then it is a sign of disappointments.

CROSS: This is a sign that trouble is on its way and if on the bottom of the cup then the trouble is going to be serious. A cross inside a circle indicates some type of confinement, perhaps a hospital, or the home or even imprisonment. Inside a square means that the trouble can be averted.

DASHES: A project already started, but a long way still to go.

DOTS: Generally something good on the way, usually money, although small single dots tend to represent letters, while one large dot represents a present.

LINES: Straight lines indicate definite plans whereas wavy lines mean uncertainty. If the lines are long and surrounded by dots then it is a sign of a long and monetary gain.

OBLONG: Quarrels.

SQUARE: Joy, peace and protection.

TRIANGLE: If upright it is a symbol of success but if reversed, it usually means missed opportunities and bad luck.

Numbers

Numbers turn up in the cup very often and usually supply additional information to the symbols they are in conjunction with. If they stand out alone in the cup, then they may be read as symbols in their own right.

ONE: Action and ambition; indicates immediate action to be taken to solve any problems and to take any practical opportunities for advancement, especially in business.

TWO: Balance; symbolises a time for making careful plans and to accept disappointments philosophically as good luck is on the way.

THREE: Luck and versatility; this is a time when nothing can go wrong. In business ventures, partnerships are favourable.

FOUR: Reliability; indicates a careful, methodical path to success. For gamblers, it is a sign that luck will be most unfavourable.

FIVE: Fate and adventure; this is when the most unexpected is most likely to turn up. However, don't take chances.

SIX: Conflict and reconciliation; an understanding attitude should be adopted. This is a very social number indicating the time for gatherings of all descriptions providing conflicts are avoided.

SEVEN: Lucky day; a "mysterious" period with out-of-the-ordinary happenings. A time to play hunches.

EIGHT: Big business; Everything is about to take on a larger than life attitude. Constructive efforts will bring speedy rewards.

NINE: Foundation and illusion; this number often seems to have double meanings. Opportunities never seem to be around at the right time. Now's the time to make contacts, to listen to sound advice and to announce important plans and decisions. However, use caution and be prepared for the unexpected!

Symbols and Their Meaning

ACORN: Health, wealth and happiness.
AIRCRAFT: Promotion and new projects.
ANCHOR: Travel.
ANTS: Many difficulties before success.
ANVIL: Continuous effort needed for success.
APPLE: Success.
ARCH: An unexpected happening.
ARROW: Bad news.
AXE: Danger.
BABY: New interests, but if near the handle it is a symbol of an addition to the family.
BALL: Restlessness.
BASKET: A useful gift.
BAT: Fear of authority.
BEAR: Misfortune through stupidity.
BED: Laziness.
BEES: A busy time ahead.
BELL: Promotion. A happy marriage.
BIRDS: Good news and good luck.
BIRD CAGE: Confinement and frustration.
BOAT: Desire for travel and discovery.
BOOT: A new home.
BOOK: New information.
BOTTLE: Illness.
BOUQUET: Happiness.
BOX: Uncertainty.
BRACELET: Gathering of friends.
BRANCH: New friendships or a birth.
BRIDGE: Problems soon to be solved.
BROOM: New beginnings.
BUILDING: Desire for new home or job.
BULL: Quarrels ahead.
BUTTERFLY: Pleasure and happy times around the corner.
CABBAGE: Envy.
CAGE: A proposal.
CAR: Change of surroundings.
CASTLE: A wish fulfilled.
CAT: False friends and deceit.
CHAIN: News of a marriage.
CHAIR: Time to take it easy.
CHICKEN: Ability.
CHILD: Innocence.
CHURCH: Faith.
CLOCK: Illness.
CLOUDS: Problems and doubts.
CLOVER: Luck.
CLOWN: Simple pleasures.
COFFIN: Failure, bad news, sometimes means a death.
COMET: Sudden and unexpected happenings.

COMPASS: Travel and new directions in life.
COW: Prosperity.
CRAB: Interference in your love life.
CRADLE: Children.
CROW: Trouble on its way.
CROWN: Success, often through sheer luck rather than effort.
CYMBAL: Be cautious, especially in matters concerning love.
CUP: Happiness, a new friend.
DAGGER: Danger.
DAFFODIL: Success and great wealth. Hope.
DAISY: Simplicity. Easy acquisition of lovers.
DEER: Arguments if not careful.
DOG: True friendship.
DONKEY: Patience.
DOOR: An unexpected and unusual event.
DOVE: Messenger of love.
DRAGON: A new beginning.
DRUM: Time for a change.
DUCK: Persistent effort needed in matters concerning money.
EAGLE: Elevation, attainment and fame.
EAR: Pleasant news.
EARRING: Luxury to come.
EASLE: Opportunity to learn new skills.
EGG: Good luck and success.
ELEPHANT: Past help remembered.
ENGINE: Journey.
EYE: Be on the look-out for an unexpected opportunity.
FACE: Friends.
FAIRY: Romance on the way.
FAN: Flirtations.

FEATHER: Fantastic good luck. The larger the feather the greater the luck.
FERN: Restlessness.
FISH: Luck in gambling.
FLAG: Trouble ahead.
FLIES: Petty annoyances.
FLOWERS: Tokens of love and affection.
FOUNTAIN: Everlasting love.
FOX: A deceitful friend.
FROG: Changes bringing advancement.
FRUIT: Ambition satisfied.
GATE: Problems.
GLASSES: Caution needed.
GOAT: Stubborn enemies.
GRASS: Ease and luxury in life.
GRIFFIN: Accident.
GUN: Quarrels to be avoided.
HAMMER: Hard work soon to be rewarded.
HAND: Help from a friend.
HARE: Sadness.
HARP: Romance.
HAT: Fame.
HEART: Love and happiness.
HIVE: Future prospoerity.
HORN: Abundance.
HORSE: A lover.
HORSESHOE: Good luck. A time to push ahead with plans.
HOURGLASS: Decisions.
HOUSE: Success.
INITIALS: These represent people who you know or will know.
INKWELL: A letter containing good news.
IVY: True love.
JEWEL: A legacy.
JOCKEY: Gambling.
JUG: Extravagance.
KETTLE: Home comforts.
KEY: Something to your advantage.
KITE: High ambitions will need perseverance.
KNIFE: Illness.
LADDER: Success and prosperity ahead.
LAMP: Celebrations.
LEAF: A letter.
LEAVES: Hope, happiness and many lovers.
LETTERS: News.
LOAF: Domestic happiness.
LOCK: Obstacles.
MAN: A visitor.
MASK: Insincerity.
MERMAID: Temptation.
MITRE: Deserved fame.

MOON: Romance is around the corner.
MOUNTAIN: Difficult time ahead.
MOUSE: Theft.
MUSHROOM: Mental or physical disturbance.
NAIL: Pain.
NECKLACE: Success.
NEEDLE: Trouble followed by joy.
NOSE: A great discovery.
NUN: Confinement.
NURSE: Illness.
NUMBERS: Time—days or weeks.
OAK: Long life and happiness.
OWL: Trouble and loss.
OYSTER: A long engagement.
PAIL: Hard work in marriage but much love.
PALM TREE: A happy and contented life.
PARCEL: A gift.
PARROT: Gossip.
PEACOCK: Luxury and vanity.
PIG: Mixture of good and bad luck.
PIPE: Long life and happiness.
PURSE: Money.
RACKET: Invitations.
RATTLE: Many children.
RAVEN: Trouble caused by gossip.
RING: A wedding.
ROSE: Luck in life and love.
SAW: Hard work.
SAUCER: Contented married life.
SCALES: Involvement with the law.
SCEPTRE: Authority.
SCISSORS: Quarrels.
SCYTHE: Danger.
SHIP: Travel.
SNAKE: Trouble and misfortune.
SPADE: Wealth through steady work.
SPIDER: Unexpected money.
STAR: Joy and prosperity.
SPOON: A christening.
SUN: Health, wealth and happiness.
SWAN: A lover.
SWORD: Arguments and problems in home and business affairs.
TEA-POT: Discussions.
TENT: Time for a rest.
TELESCOPE: Plan for the future.
THISTLE: Happy, though never rich.
TOAD: Time to drop those hangers-on.
TORTOISE: Difficulties eventually overcome.
TREE: Good health.
TRIDENT: Success with anything connected with the sea.

TRUNK: Happiness at the end of a journey.
UMBRELLA: Good luck through friendships.
VASE: Good deeds will bring future rewards.
VIOLETS: Love.
WALL: A lover's tiff.
WATCH: A secret admirer.
WHEEL: Promotion.
WINDMILL: Enterprise.
WINGS: Messages.
WOLF: Greed.
WOMAN: Happy family.
ZEBRA: A foreign country or a foreign lover.

A Sample Reading

The following is an example of how to interpet the symbols and to form them into a short story. However, you will probably not get so many symbols all at the same time in one cup. Recognition and accuracy is the main thing.

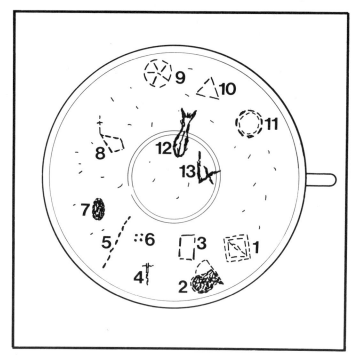

The GATE (1) to the left of the handle indicates that there have been problems in the past, while the JUG (2) and the OBLONG (3) symbolise that there have been many extravagances which have probably led to quarrels. The number ONE (4) indicates that immediate action must be taken to solve the problems and any practical opportunities must be taken. The STRAIGHT LINE (5) surrounded by the DOTS (6) mean that definite plans for monetary gain have been formulated, while the EGG (7) foretells of good luck and success in all projects.

The KITE (8) shows that perseverance is needed to obtain the high ambitions and that promotion, the WHEEL (9), is in the not too distant future. The TRIANGLE (10) again indicates success and the CIRCLE (11) adds the further assurance of complete and continuing happiness. However, the FISH (12) and the number FOUR (4) at the bottom of the cup warns that Lady Luck is not in a good mood and that any gambling will not be successful and is likely to reactivate all the problems of the present time.

Coffee Grounds

The reading of coffee-grounds is exactly the same as for tea-leaves. The symbols tend to be rather more obscure, however and for this reason are thought to be not such a good medium for fortune telling. It has been found that coffee-grounds give a very spiritual reading and reveal secrets pertaining to the soul rather than the mundane events of daily life. So, if you wish to consult your cup on the higher things of life via the coffee-grounds, it is advisable to get your clairvoyant intuition working accurately by perfecting the art of tea-leaf reading first and then graduating to the coffee-grounds. Whatever you intend to do with your newly developed talent of tasseography remember, that the more you practise the better your results. Good luck and may you find fortune in your cup.

Meanings of the symbols

Acorns
An excellent symbol. The good fortune it foretells varies according to its position in the cup:
near the top – financial success
towards the middle – good health
near the bottom – improvement either in health or finances

Aircraft
A sudden journey, unexpected and not without risk
alternatively there will be a rise to new heights
if the aircraft seems broken – danger threatens, either physically or in one's career

Alligator
Treachery lies in wait

Anchor
Success awaits. Again the position in the cup is important:
at the top of the cup – success in business, augmented by the support of a faithful love
towards the middle – a voyage ending in prosperity (increased if dots surround the symbol)
at the bottom – good fortune socially. If the symbol is obscured – anticipate difficulties

Ant
With perseverance, success will arrive

Arc
Ill health threatens either career or other plans, projects may be abandoned, accidents threaten

Arrow
Bad news is on the way

Axe
Difficulties face you, especially if only the axe-head appears

Baby
Many small worries threaten
alternatively, there may be an addition to the family

Bag
A trap awaits, likely to be successful if the bag is closed

Ball
Variable fortunes await you in life

Basket
A very good sign. Again pay attention to its position:
near the handle – a baby will soon be announced
near the top of the cup – your possessions will be added to
if flowers lie in the basket – a very good sign, suggesting happiness, social success, parties and festivities
if the basket is surrounded by dots – finances will be unexpectedly augmented, perhaps by a legacy

Bat
Beware of plots and of false friends

Bear
Irrational decisions will bring difficulties and even danger in their train
if the bear is turned away from the handle a long journey is indicated

Bed
if neat – a tidy mind
if disordered – an undisciplined mind which leads to problems

Bee
Success, both social and financial; good news
near the handle – a gathering of friends
a swarm of bees – possible success with an audience

Bell
News is expected, good or bad according to the significance of the surrounding symbols
near the top of the cup – promotion
near the bottom of the cup – sad news
two bells – great joy

Bird
This is particularly lucky if there are two or more birds
flying birds – good news
standing birds – a successful voyage

Boat
Refuge in time of trouble

Book
If the book is open expect litigation, if closed difficult researches

Boot
Protection from pain
pointing away from the handle – sudden removal, perhaps dismissal
broken – failure and disgrace threaten

Bottle
Take care of health

Bridge
Opportunity to be seized for short-cut to success

Broom
Small worries disappear

Butterfly
Frivolous but innocent pleasure
if surrounded by dots this indicates the frittering away of wealth

Cabbage
Jealousy entails complications

Candle
Helpfulness, zeal for education

Castle
Strong character, rising to position of authority

Cat
Someone lies in treacherous ambush, probably a false friend

Chair
Improvement and, if the chair is surrounded by dots, financial improvement

Circle
A successful outcome

Clock
Avoid delay and hesitation
alternatively – recovery from illness
in the bottom of the cup – a death

Clouds
Doubts, unsolved problems
if the clouds are very heavy, misfortune is indicated

Column
Success. Also a danger of resultant arrogance

Comet
A visitor from overseas

Cross
Suffering, sacrifice, tribulation. Two crosses indicate severe illness or other major affliction

Crown
Great success
If the crown is neat expect a legacy

Dagger
Impetuosity
alternatively – the dangerous plotting of enemies

Dog
Rely on friends
Pay attention to the position and attitude of the dog:
running – good news and happy meetings
subdued – you may be slandering a friend
at the bottom of the cup – a friend is in trouble

Dot
A single dot emphasizes the meaning of the symbol it is nearest to. Dots in groups indicate money

Drum
Scandal and gossip threatens. Quarrels are in the air

Egg
Prosperity, success, fertility. The more eggs the better

Elephant
Wisdom, strength and slow, but solid, success

Eye
Take care and be watchful, especially in business

Feather
Instability and lack of concentration

Fence
Limitation imposed on plans and activities

Fern
Unfaithfulness is possible in a lover

Fir tree
Success, especially in the arts. The higher the tree the better

Fire
Avoid over-hasty reactions, especially anger

Fish
One of the very best omens, this indicates good luck in everything

Flag
Danger threatens, particularly if the flag is black

Flower
A wish will be granted

Fly
Worry, especially domestic. The more flies there are the more varied the swarm of misfortunes

Forked line
Decisions must be taken. (Whether these will be successful or not depends upon the attendant symbols)

Frog
Avoid self-importance as it may cause trouble

Fruit
This is a lucky symbol, especially if the fruit is in season

Garland
Success and great honour

Glass
Integrity

Goat
Enemies threaten

Gun
near the handle – an attack will threaten domestic happiness
at the bottom of the cup – slander undermines the client
for military personnel – cancelled leave

Hammer
Ability to overcome obstacles and perhaps a tendency to ruthlessness

Hare
Over-timidity

Harp
Domestic harmony
for single people a harp indicates a love affair with a successful outcome

Hat
New possibilities, and probable success
if the hat is bent and holed – failure is more likely
if the hat is in the bottom of the cup – a rival

Hawk
Sudden danger threatens

Hill
Obstacle to progress. (Especially if clouds obscure it)

Horse
galloping — good news, especially from a lover
the head only — a lover

House
Secure conditions, especially in business, so a good time for new ventures
if the sign is near the handle and obscured — domestic strife or illness may threaten the family

Human figures
Consider these carefully and take your cue from their appearance, activities and the surrounding symbols

Insect
Minor worries, soon overcome

Jester
Avoid frivolity, it might be a disadvantage. A time for seriousness

Jug
Influence, enabling the client to give help to another
near the handle — excellent health

Kettle
near the handle domestic contentment
near or at the bottom of the cup — domestic strife

Key
Intelligent appraisal can see and seize new opportunities
double, or near the bottom of the cup — danger of robbery.

Knife
Separation, broken contracts, ended friendships
near the handle — divorce
crossed knives — bitter argument

Ladder
Promotion, probably through hard work

Leaf
News
if the leaves are in clusters — happiness and good fortune

Letter
News
if obscured — bad news
if near dots — news concerning financial affairs

Light-house
Trouble threatens but will be averted before it strikes

Lines
Progress, especially if clear and straight

Lion
Influential friends and consequent success

Lock
Obstacle to your advancement

Man
near the handle — a visitor
with arm outstretched — bearing gifts

Mask
Take care, people are trying to deceive you

Mermaid
Take care, people are trying to tempt you

Monkey
Flatterers represent danger; they intend mischief

Monster
In any shape or form this indicates terror

Moon
full — a love affair
in first quarter — new projects
in last quarter — a decline in fortune
obscured — depression
surrounded by dots — marriage for money

Mountains
High ambition which will be successful if the peaks are very clear

Mushroom
Growth, expansion
near the handle — a new home in the country

Nail
Malice threatens and injustice may be inflicted

Necklace
complete – many supporters and admirers
broken – marriage or love affair may break up

Net
Beware of traps

Nurse
Illness threatens
if near the handle – dependants may fall sick

Owl
This evil omen indicates that new ventures will fail
at the bottom of the cup – disease and financial failure
near the handle – unfaithfulness destroys domestic harmony

Palm
Success, honour and respect

Parachute
Escape from danger

Parcel
This is represented by an oblong leaf and indicates a surprise. (The surrounding symbols will offer a clue as to the nature of the surprise)

Parrot
Scandal and gossip threaten

Peacock
with tail spread – possession of an estate
surrounded by dots – a life of luxurious ease
near a ring – a rich marriage

Pear
Comfort and financial ease

Pentagon
Mental and intellectual balance

Pig
Mixed fortune. (Material success may bring spiritual or psychological disaster)

Pistol
Danger, perhaps moral danger, threatens

Pot
Service to society

Profile
Temporary friendship, or acquaintanceship

Pump
A generous nature

Purse
Profit, usually material
at the bottom of the cup – this indicates an unexpected loss

Question mark
Hesitancy

Rabbit
Timidity

Rake
Attempts should be made to tidy things up and regulate life-style and work methods

Rat
Treachery and loss, deceitful friends and resourceful enemies

Reptile
Treachery and malice threaten, especially from false friends

Ring
Self-sufficiency, completion, eternity
near the top of the cup – a marriage is indicated
near the middle – marriage is offered
at the bottom – a long engagement (but if a cross is nearby it is doomed to be broken)
two rings – plans come to fruition, projects work out

Saw
Outsiders will threaten domestic tranquillity

Scales
A lawsuit is likely
balanced scales – justice will be done
unbalanced scales – injustice will be suffered

Scissors
Separation, quarrelling
near the handle – domestic bickering

Ship
Good fortune and/or good tidings are on their way

Skeleton
Ill health, poverty

Snake
Hatred and enmity, vicious plots

Spade
Hard work, but success at the end of it

Spider
This indicates a determined, persistent character (but with some guile and cunning)

Square
Restriction, even imprisonment: either external, of the body; or internal, of the mind

Star
six-pointed – good fortune
eight-pointed – a bad omen, accidents and reverses may be suffered
five stars – success, but no joy
seven stars – grief

Sun
Great happiness, success and power

Swallow
Swiftness of decision
This also indicates unexpected journeys, leading to a happy outcome

Swan
Smooth and contented life

Table
Dinner, party, feast, social gathering
dots nearby – a conference on financial matters

Toad
Beware of flattery and flatterers

Tortoise
Over-sensitivity to criticism

Trees
Plans will be fruitful, ambitions fulfilled

Triangle
pointing upwards – success
pointing downwards – plans go awry

Trunk
A journey and fateful decisions

Umbrella
Shelter will be needed
if the umbrella is open it will be found,
if closed, denied

Violin
Individualism, perhaps egoism

Volcano
Passions may erupt and cause harm

Vulture
Loss, perhaps through theft; danger, possibly from an enemy in authority

Whale
Pre-eminence and success, especially in business

Windmill
Success will be achieved through industry and hard work, not brilliance

Wings
News is expected. (The attendant symbols will suggest whether this will be good or bad)

Woman
Happiness and pleasure
more than one woman, scandal and gossip

Yoke
Domination threatens, so avoid being too submissive

Zebra
Adventures overseas. (An unsettled life is indicated)

RADIESTHESIA AND DOWSING

What exactly is radiesthesia? The word is an anglicised form of the French word *radiesthesie* and means the perception of radiation. The term is used generally to cover all phenomena that come under the category of dowsing, although practising dowsers would tend to disagree. To them, dowsing generally applies to the use of the rod for water or mineral divining whereas radiesthesia covers mainly the diagnosis of disease with the pendulum. The history of dowsing disappears into the mists of time, but almost certainly Neolithic man used it for detecting suitable sites for his sacred structures. If modern man did the same, perhaps his buildings would stay up a little longer. After all Stonehenge has been standing for 4,000 years and we have nothing to compete with it, either in size or permanency.

What is happening on the dowsing scene today? Is it really worth learning or should it be buried in the past? Dowsing and radiesthesia are still as relevant today and probably more useful than ever. In Vietnam, the U.S. marines have used it to locate tunnels, booby traps and sunken mortar shells, etc. In Russia they used to call it the wizard's rod, but now large scale investigations are being carried out by geophysicists, geologists and physiologists at the Moscow and Leningrad Geological Institutes. In Russia dowsing is now a legitimate scientific field of research with a brand new modern name — B.P.E. — Biophysical Effects Method, and the rod is claimed to be the "simplest of all conceivable electrophysiological instruments". So if you want to learn to dowse or to be a radiesthesist — go ahead — you're in good company. Though ancient kings are no longer practical examples to follow, few people would argue with a valid scientific field, and if you think the words dowsing or radiesthesia are too out of date to use, you can always baffle your friends with science and talk about the Biophysical Effects Method.

Pendulums or Rods?

First things first; whether to use a pendulum or a rod and how to go about getting them. The first is a matter of preference and also practicalities. For instance, try finding water in an open field on a windy day with a pendulum and you'll soon get the picture. Pendulums are very convenient and are small enough to carry around. I know of more than one person who is never without one and as soon as they want help solving a problem, get curious about the situation they find themselves in, or just feel a little bored — out comes the pendulum and they're away. Pendulums vary a great deal; they can either be made of ivory, plastic, beechwood, etc., and come in a variety of shapes and sizes, from large spheres to long pointed ones and small round ones. Many of them are hollow so you can put a sample in, but this is not necessary. For those just starting out, a simple glass bead on a piece of cotton is just as

Left: *This woodcut from Agricola's book on mining of 1580 shows men using rods to discover metal.* **Below:** *An anxious crowd watch the blindfold dowser try to locate an underground of spring.*

good. Most of the companies who manufacture pendulums seem very reluctant to send out price lists — perhaps they don't want customers?

Rods are a little more difficult to get hold of so you will probably have to make your own. If you intend to be a real enthusiast you can make yourself a genuine hazel rod, but here again you can improvise, one man I know has one he made out of old corset stays that works extremely well. You can easily make your own out of two metal coathangers. First untwist the metal around the hook and straighten the whole thing out as best as possible. Cut off the hook and the other twisted end, and then bend one end at right angles until you have something that looks like a "L". Bend about eight inches so that you will have a comfortable length to hold. Make two of these and you have a set of divining rods. Next you will want to know how to hold the pendulum or rod. The pendulum is held between the thumb and first finger by the cotton or by the little handle if you have a professional looking one. The two rods are held one in each hand. Whatever position you are in try to make it as comfortable as possible so there will be no distractions such as aching arms and cramp.

There are various "rules" affecting rods and pendulums such as the length of string and elbows and arms to be held clear of the body. Ignore all the rules for the length of string, it is a personal thing and all you have to do is to find the length that gives you the best movement and then stick to it. It may be three inches long or ten inches long, but use whatever is best for you. When using the rod you should hold your arms straight out, but this is very tiring and not altogether necessary unless it's the only way it will work for you. Try practising with your arms in various bent positions until you find the right one and the one which is comfortable to use. If you are not comfortable you are wasting your time! Another rule is not to start the pendulum swinging. However, in some cases, if you don't,

Below: *This illustration from Abbe de Villemont's* Traite de la Physique Occulte, *1693, demonstrates some different forms of dowsing rods, and the various methods of holding them.*

you could be waiting all day for something to happen. When asking questions start the pendulum by giving it a little push — it will soon settle down and make its own movement. When dowsing on maps wait for the pendulum to make its own reaction over whatever you are looking for. If you follow your own intuition in these matters your sensitivity will increase and your results will be much more accurate.

Finding Your Polarity

When using your pendulum, you will find that it makes several movements, a clockwise circle, an anti-clockwise circle, swing, which is technically called oscillation or not move at all. Before you start to use it you have to know what your polarity is. This simply means if the pendulum circles clockwise for a positive answer and counter-clockwise for a negative answer or vice-versa. The easiest way to determine this is to hold the pendulum in your right hand and ask a question that you know can only be answered as "Yes". For example, "Is my name John?" Give the pendulum a gentle push and when it has settled down note which way it is forming the circle. If clockwise, you are positively polarised, if anti-clockwise, you are negatively polarised. As a check you should then ask it a question that can only be answered with a "No". If you are a positive person it will circle anti-clockwise and if you are a negative person it will circle clockwise. If it goes the same way as previously — you're in trouble. Try to concentrate a little more and you should soon get good results.

Another way of finding your polarity is to hold the pendulum over the positive (north-seeking) pole of a magnet. If it circles clockwise you are a "positive" person and if it circles anti-clockwise you are negatively polarised. This polarisation has absolutely nothing to do with anything but your reactions with a pendulum. Either males or females can be negatively or positively polarised. With the rod, when positively polarised, it will react by dipping over the positive pole of the magnet and rising over the negative.

All matter, whether a stone, a plant or a human being is composed of atoms and these atoms are constantly vibrating and giving off energy or radiations. There are many different types of radiation and everything has its own specific radiation. The radiations of water are quite different from those of gold, and every human being has his or her own special vibration which is theirs alone. Most people are sensitive to these radiations in some way or other. The dowser merely uses the pendulum or rod as a type of aerial for amplifying these vibrations, so that the radiesthesic or dowsing faculty is an extension of the sense of touch, as clairvoyance is the extension of seeing, clairaudience the extension of hearing, etc. In a sense, the body is just like a television set; as the aerial on the roof of the house, or wherever, picks up the transmissions that are being beamed through the air from the T.V. studio, it channels them down through the wire and into the set where they are reconstituted into pictures on the screen.

Keep an Open Mind

If you are looking for gold, the metal will be giving off its specific "gold" vibrations. When using the rod or the pendulum your body will pick up these radiations which will then be translated into a movement of the rod so that it virtually says. "Gold is down there". A similar thing happens when asking the pendulum questions. The sub-conscious knows the answer to your questions because in a sense it functions outside time and space and when answering the questions of friends it is in contact with their subconsciousnesses telepathically. If all this sounds a bit way-out or far-fetched try to keep an open mind on the subject and try using the pendulum. You will soon see that it works and if you are not satisfied with this definition of how it works, then try to work it out for yourself either logically or with the pendulum. If you clog your mind with doubts then radiesthesia will not work for you so just keep an open mind or, if you must, find an answer that suits you.

Before you get started, here are a few hints that might help you. When using the pendulum, don't smoke at the same time as you need all your concentration for the pendulum. Washing the hands before you start does seem to help some people as it clears away any extraneous influences. Try to keep away from metal objects and electric currents as these can interfere and give false readings. Don't try to do too much at one time. Concentrate on what you are asking and try not to let your mind wander.

Cultivate Indifference

When asking questions about yourself you must

be completely indifferent. If you cannot be, then you should get a friend to help you and ask your question silently whilst your friend holds the pendulum. In that way, your friend's attitude cannot affect the answer to your question because she doesn't know what it is and you can't affect it because you're not holding the pendulum. Some people can make the pendulum move the way they want it to even if another person is holding it, by concentrating intently on the answer they want and so transferring it to the pendulum. So if you want the correct answer be careful. When wanting to know a time factor, ask questions like "Will this happen next week, month, year, in October, etc.?" Be specific and your questions will always be correct. The more you use your pendulum the more sensitive your whole body will become and you will actually begin to "feel" the vibration within your body before it is translated to the pendulum.

Advanced Dowsing

This section does not mean advanced in the sense of being very difficult, it merely means that there are more instructions to remember and more factors to be taken into consideration. *Shape* is the first consideration; two- or three-dimensional geometric figures produce deviations in the magnetic fields of the earth so that it is not the object that is detected but the effect it produces. Spheres and cubes, etc., give out emissions in different directions, so it is very important to know the object's shape when dowsing so that you can allow for the effect. To make this a little clearer, if you draw a rectangle 4 inches by 7 inches and, holding the pendulum about two inches above the line, follow along the seven inch side. At first the pendulum will oscillate — swing along the line and then it will suddenly swing at right angles. If you then measure from the beginning of the line to the point where the pendulum crossed it, you will find that it measures four inches, and that you have marked out a square. Try the same thing with a circle and you will find that the pendulum will divide it into ten sections.

Colour also has various effects on the pendulum. It will react in a positive manner above the colours red, orange and yellow, negatively over blue, violet and indigo — the cool colours of the spectrum — and make a curious neither positive nor negative movement above green, which is

the middle of the spectrum. Try putting coloured pieces of paper inside a number of envelopes and see the reaction. Colour can help you enormously in your detection although it limits you to finding only the objects that give out the same vibration as the colour. Try finding various objects in a room flooded with different coloured light and see what results you get.

Red Herrings

Other complications appear in the form of *Remonance*, *Parasitic images* and *Telluric emissions*. Sounds complicated doesn't it but it really isn't once you know exactly what they are. As I have already said, everything gives off radiations and some of these are left behind when an object is moved to another place. These remaining "red herrings" vibrations can lead you a merry song and dance if you are not careful but with practice and if you listen to your intuition you should be able to tell which is the correct reading and which is the remonance.

Below: *Another early woodcut illustrates the possibilities of dowsing for discovering metal deposits. It appeared in Sebastian Munster's* Cosmography *published in 1550.*

Parasitic images usually occur when searching for water or minerals. A sensitive person is very prone to these little tricks of nature as they are reflections from a large object to a similar small object. When looking for various ores and the find is not as large as was expected, then parasitic reflections have been at work and you have to try again. To overcome this you place a metal circle on the ground with a sample of what you are looking for in the centre and another sample in your hand. The object will register in the middle of the circle and in one other place, that being where it actually is.

Telluric emissions are those of the soils caused mainly by geological faults and are often harmful. The only way to distinguish between these emissions and those of say underground water is to dowse an area with a sample of water in one hand and a pendulum in the other and note both your reactions and the pendulum's over a spot with water. Then go over the same ground without the sample and note your different reactions. Only by this trial and error method can you learn to distinguish between vibrations.

So, now you have all the equipment and know what you're doing, it's time to start some practical investigations. Most people who practise dowsing have certain preferences to the type of work they do. Some only divine for water, others minerals or specialise in finding lost objects. Try everything and be good at all forms or choose your favourite and specialise.

Open Air Detection

With this you can do the full water-witching process if you feel inclined, zooming across the fields with rod in hand and impressing all the curious people you are bound to attract with your science. Rods really are the best for open air work, but if you do want to use a pendulum, go ahead, only if there is a lot of wind, use a heavy one or it will make a lot of odd movements. Decide exactly what you are going to dowse for; it may be for water, mineral or oil and you should obtain a sample if possible. Some people are able to get excellent results by just visualising what they are looking for. Try this if you want to and see what happens. Just hold the thought that you want to find that certain thing as firmly and as clearly as you can, then you are all ready to start.

With the sample held in your hand along with the rod, start walking up and down your selected area in a methodical manner. If you use the traditional forked twig you can suspend the sample from where the two handles join. As you find what you are looking for the rod will dip or rise according to your polarity or if you are using

Below: *There was a fashionable interest in dowsing during the 17th century, as the gentlemanly costume of this dowser indicates. From Abbe de Villemont,* Traite de la Physique Occulte.

the coathanger improvisation the two rods will cross. As long as you have taken all the "problems" into consideration your divination should be accurate.

When looking for water, the rod will dip over a standing pool of water and rise over running water if you are positively polarised. If it is running water you will be able to find the direction it flows by trying to follow it; going up-stream the rod will lift and will dip going down-stream if you are a "positive". The usual method of finding the depth of the water is complicated so it is best to make a little apparatus called a coil to help you. Use an insulated rod about eight inches long, of glass or wood, etc., and half an inch in diameter. Wrap around it a length of copper wire, about 19 gauge, then form the remainder into a twelve inch long and six inch wide loop, closing back at the rod. You can now either remove the rod or leave it in according to your preference. Test the coil over water; it should dip and rotate.

When you have found your water in the field, take the coil and stand over the flow; the coil should be drawn downwards and then start to rotate. Each rotation corresponds to approximately two feet in depth. The coil will then stop for a moment and indicate the direction of the current, then it will rotate the opposite way and indicate the volume. The detection of minerals and oil is similar with extra little hazards. For example, "positive" people can quite easily detect gold, copper and diamonds, but "negative" people cannot detect diamonds even though they may be able to find coal. You never know what you can do until you try.

Map Detection
This is again quite easy and it is a good idea to locate your water, etc., on a map before you actually dowse the area. Always use a good printed map to prevent errors and if you are using plans of houses, etc., make them as accurate as possible and to a suitable scale. Allow for all the little tricks of nature and if possible work with a sample, if you are detecting water or minerals, etc. Orientate the map in a north-south direction if possible as this makes it a little easier to tune into the vibrations accurately. Don't work on a table with drawers because their shape will create all sorts of odd images and either sit or stand in a comfortable

position. Do not let others touch you or the map when you are working as this will disturb and confuse the radiations you are trying to detect. Remember, you are working with the earth's magnetic field and your own powers of detection.

Always use good samples. If you are looking for water in chalky areas it is no use using a sample of water from a pure spring. Using samples of iron, railways can be followed; using an electric battery you can locate power cables. Working with a map is much easier and more convenient than dowsing in the open as many of the adverse influences can be avoided. Always place the sample on the northern edge of the map.

Missing Persons
When trying to find missing persons by using a map, you will need a photograph, preferably a recent one that has not been handled too much. Concentrate on finding only the person in the photograph. At first you will encounter many parasitic images that will throw you off the

correct track, but with practice you should become almost perfect. Missing animals can also be traced this way.

Even the police have been known to employ dowsers to find missing criminals and people. Unfortunately many missing persons turn up dead and it is the body that has to be traced, so if you are going to do something of this sort it is wise to see if they are still alive using your pendulum. Practise asking the pendulum whether people are still living or not with photographs of historical figures, etc. For me the pendulum circles positively over a live male and negatively over one who is no longer living. Over a live female it swings negatively but over a dead female it circles positively. But find out your own guide lines.

Finding lost objects is a little difficult as

Left: *A water diviner at work.* **Below left:** *the rod is being held in the normal position.* **Below right:** *The downward position of the rod indicates that water has been found.*

usually no sample is available. Also by using pieces of the material it is made of, say for finding a lost gold ring set with diamonds, rubies and emeralds you used a sample of each, you would probably locate any object having one or more of those minerals. The best thing to do is to draw the lost object as accurately as possible and then add samples of the stones and metal if possible. Using this method you will be able to obtain about 90% accuracy.

Archaeological Dowsing

As I said at the beginning of this chapter, the ancients were very keen dowsers and put their knowledge to very practical things such as siting buildings, etc. Guy Underwood, in his book *The Pattern of the Past* has explored this subject in great detail so if this line of dowsing appeals to you I suggest you try to read it. He believes that ancient man sited his religious constructions using water divining so that they could always be rediscovered by this means. So far, it has been discovered by various people that burial mounds and similar stone structures appear to be surrounded by underground streams; stone avenues such as at Carnac are aligned upon parallel underground streams, while many other prehistoric sites are crossed by these underground streams. Many prehistoric sites have been discovered by dowsing so if it appeals to you start looking. Practise first on *known* sites first using a map, and then if possible by visiting the area. When you are proficient you can try to discover unknown sites.

Are You Living in a Haunted House?

Many people who move into a new house often find strange things happening to them. After eliminating all the possible explanations they can think of, the inevitable question arises, "Is the house haunted?" Some of the experiences include strange dreams, loss of energy, sleeplessness, odd noises and depressive feelings.

If you think your house is haunted draw an accurate diagram of the house and by asking specific questions try to locate the area that is being haunted. Once located, try to find out exactly what it is. If the spirit of a dead person, why is it still there? Is it an animal spirit, or is it a collection of negative thoughts and images? Rooms that have been the scene of unpleasant happenings often retain the vibrations of fear, despair, gloom, etc., even if they are not actually haunted by some spirit. If you believe your house is haunted, then you have a problem as it might be difficult to remove it and if you can't find someone to clear it you may end up having to live with it as best you can. On the other hand it may not be a ghost but a natural phenomena caused by underground water.

There are many ways of using the dowsing or radiesthesic faculty and I'm sure that once you've started to use your pendulum or rod many practical ideas will occur to you. Learn to detect arithmetical errors or forgeries. Learn to tell character from handwriting using a pendulum. If it oscillates perpendicularly across the writing, the person has a very good character; swinging from side to side along the writing indicated a normally good character, but if it changes and begins to swing in an ellipse, then the person is confused. A negative reaction indicated idleness and lack of conscience; positive reactions, strangely enough, indicate a person with everything that is bad. If you do analyse handwriting in this way, remember that it is very general and if you are not careful you could be minus a few friends. So, by all means test handwriting, but don't publish the fact too much — you could also be wrong.

Do have fun with your dowsing; the more you practise the more accurate you get and the more your pendulum will become attuned to your vibrations. You have the dowsing faculty so why not make practical use of it.

Below: *Mademoiselle Martin indicating a bell under the water. Some people are gifted with an uncanny power for locating lost objects. From Figurer*, Mysteres de la Science.